# MATTHEW
## His Kingdom Forever

Let the word of Christ dwell in you richly as you teach and admonish
one another with all wisdom, and as you sing psalms, hymns and spiritual
songs with gratitude in your hearts to God (Colossians 3:16).

Written by Pauline and Leonard Erdman

Compiled by Debb Andrus

Edited by Rodney L. Rathmann

SAINT

# Contents

# Lesson 1

# The King
# (Matthew 1–2)

## Approaching This Study

**Key verses:** "Where is the one who has been born king of the Jews? We saw His star in the east and have come to worship Him" **(Matthew 2:2).**

"She will give birth to a son, and you are to give Him the name Jesus, because He will save His people from their sins" **(Matthew 1:21).**

**Aims of this lesson:** To recognize Jesus Christ as the fulfillment of the Messianic prophecies of the Old Covenant and to put our trust in Him as Savior and King.

## We Need to Belong

*Only the headlights of the car pierced the darkness of the night on the desert highway as the family returned home after a holiday in Mexico. The songs and chatter of the children had quieted down and their eyelids were becoming droopy.*

*Suddenly, out of nowhere a stop sign appeared. As the car slowed to a stop, a uniformed man appeared at the car window and asked, "Where were you born?" Each person in the car had to give proof of his or her citizenship or, if an alien, show papers to prove that he or she had the right or permission to enter the United States.*

We want to belong; we need to belong; to a kingdom, a nation. Refugees plead for some nation to accept them. The word *alien* has a cold, lonesome, frightening sound to it. The word *citizen* gives a warm feeling of belonging. An alien has little or no rights or privileges. A citizen has many rights and privileges.

We want to belong to a kingdom or nation that is lasting, not easily overthrown by rebellion from within or an enemy from without. We want peace and protection. We want a secure future for ourselves and our loved ones.

Where can we find such a kingdom?

God has promised such a kingdom and He has promised a King. The Lord spoke to Nathan. "Go," He said, "and tell My servant David, 'This is what the Lord says: . . . When your days are over and you rest with your fathers, I will raise up your offspring to succeed you, who will come from your own body, and I will establish His kingdom. He is the one who will build a house for My Name, and I will establish the throne of His kingdom forever' " (2 Samuel 7:5, 12–13). Through Isaiah, God said, "For to us a child is born, to us a son is given, and the government will be on His shoulders. And He will be called Wonderful Counselor, Mighty God, Everlasting Father, Prince of Peace. Of the increase of His government and peace there will be no end. He will reign on David's throne and over his kingdom, establishing and upholding it with justice and righteousness from that time on and forever" (Isaiah 9:6–7).

Yes, we look for a kingdom that will last forever, a kingdom of righteousness and justice and peace. But the kingdom that God promises is not a kingdom of this world. It is a spiritual kingdom, a communion of believers in union with Jesus Christ. Jesus Christ is the Head, the King, and the blessings of this kingdom are the sum total of all the gifts of God in Christ Jesus as they are enjoyed here on earth in the Christian church and, finally above, in the kingdom of glory.

# Working with the Text

## The Genealogy of the King

Read **Matthew 1:1–17.** (Don't feel badly if you have trouble pronouncing some of those names. Most everyone does!)

1. How did Matthew get immediately to Christ, the King, in **verse 1?** Also see **Psalm 89:3–4.**

*A record of the genealogy of Jesus Christ the son of David, the son of Abraham*

2. Why was Abraham mentioned in **verse 2?** (See **Genesis 12:1–3.**)

*Abraham was the beginning of God's blessing & promise on all to follow*

3. What is a genealogy? Why is Christ's genealogy so important?

*Genealogy = Lineage. God's promises (a Savior + salvation) are linked to Christ & ∴ fulfillment*

4. What do these verses tell us about God's promises?

*God keeps His promises*

Notice that Christ's genealogy in Matthew is traced through His foster father, Joseph. Both Joseph and Mary were descendants of David. For Jews, the lines of legal descent were traced through males. Matthew's genealogy points to Christ as both the son of royalty and the son of promise.

## The Birth of the King

Read **Matthew 1:18–25.**

1. What was unusual about Jesus' conception?

*Mary was found to be w/child through the Holy Spirit*

2. Where can you find reference to the Trinity in these verses?

*fulfill what the Lord said; they will call him Immanuel — which meant "God with us"*

3. Notice that God works in unusual ways. The fact that Jesus was conceived by the Holy Spirit makes Jesus Christ one of a kind. How would you describe Him?

*Jesus Christ was a miraculous representation b/c he was both God & man*

4. *Angel* means "messenger." What was the message from God to Joseph? What motivated Joseph to change his plans?

*God sent an angel to tell Joseph not to be afraid that Mary conceived thru the Holy Spirit & a son wld be born to save the people from their sins. Joseph obeyed.*

5. What does the name *Jesus* mean?

*Immanuel — God with us*

6. The nature of sin is to separate us from God. How would Jesus save His people? (See **Isaiah 53:5–6** and **John 1:29**.)

*Jesus was the sacrifice who atoned for our sins. Jesus suffered our punishment on the cross.*

7. Matthew quotes **Isaiah 7:14**. Notice that the birth of Jesus Christ took place according to God's plan. What does the name *Immanuel* teach us about Jesus?

*The name Immanuel teaches us that God is with us — that Jesus is God.*

8. Why is the teaching of the virgin birth of Jesus so important? Could Jesus be our Savior without being God?

*The virgin birth fulfills God's plan for salvation. It shows that Jesus is God. No*

# Wise Men Visit the King

Read **Matthew 2:1–12.**

1. Why did the Wise Men come to Jerusalem?

*The Magi were following a star in the east. They went to Jerusalem b/c it was capital city of Judaism + they were looking for the king of the Jews to worship him.*

2. Why would Herod get so upset at the mention of the birth of a king of the Jews? *Herod feared anyone who might threaten his being king. b/c he was a non-Jew who was appointed*

3. How did the Jewish religious leaders know that the promised King would be born in Bethlehem? (See **Micah 5:2**.) *They knew the promised King wld be born in Bethlehem b/c of the prophecy in Micah eleven centuries earlier.*

4. What was the significance of the star? (See **Numbers 24:17**.) *Num 24:17 says that Israel's future Deliverer will be like a star. The Magi were led to Jesus by his star.*

5. How did the Wise Men worship the infant King? *The Magi bowed down & worshiped him. They presented gifts of gold, incense & myrrh. They returned another rte bypassing Herod.*

6. What evidences of the Wise Men's faith do you find in this chapter? *The Wise Men followed a star; they worshiped Jesus & brought him gifts; they protected Jesus from Herod.*

# The King Escapes and Returns

Read **Matthew 2:13–23**.

1. Give examples of God's protection and care of the infant King from these verses. *God sent an angel to Joseph telling him to flee to Egypt; when Herod died, God sent an angel telling Joseph to go to Israel; went to Nazareth when heard about Archelaus*

2. Notice the opposition to the kingdom of Jesus Christ already in these verses. Why did Herod oppose His kingdom? Why do people oppose His kingdom today? *Herod opposed Jesus b/c he thought Jesus was a threat to his kingdom. People oppose today b/c don't want to follow God's will & the Word & want own way.*

# Applying the Message

1. When I acknowledge Jesus as my Savior, it means that I…

*acknowledge Jesus is the son of God - I was chosen to be his own by the Holy Spirit - Jesus died for my sins*

When I acknowledge Jesus as my King, it means that I…

*know Jesus is the same yesterday, today + tomorrow - Jesus keeps his promises*

2. The birth of Jesus was a fulfillment of prophecy. What does the fulfillment of prophecy mean to me?

*God keeps His promises*

3. Wise Men and wisdom go together. How can I be wise like the Wise Men? (Consider the faith of the Wise Men.)

*Through faith + by following God's will, not mine*

4. Identify examples of Mary and Joseph's faith. How does their faith speak to me today?

*Mary + Joseph never lost faith in God — they obeyed Him.*

5. I will share the Good News of Jesus Christ, my Savior and King, with others in the following ways:

*By example*
*By studying the Word +*
*gaining more knowledge so I'm*
*prepared to answer questions*

# Closing Prayer Suggestion

King Jesus, You are everything we want and hope for. You give us peace because God the Father is no longer angry over our sins. You have taken them away. You bring us justice and righteousness because what is Yours, a holy life, You have given to us, and what is ours, death and punishment, You have taken upon Yourself. You give us security because we know that neither Satan nor death nor anything else can destroy Your kingdom. Thank You for accepting us through faith as citizens in Your kingdom. We want Your loving rule in our lives. Amen.

# Taking the Lesson Home

1. Study Advent and Christmas hymns. Note references to the King and the Kingdom.

2. Matthew refers to the Scriptures of the Old Covenant many times in his gospel. Study the prophecies and their fulfillment using Bible dictionaries, commentaries, and concordances.

3. Study the women mentioned in the genealogy of **Matthew 1:** Tamar **(Genesis 38),** Rahab **(Joshua 2; Hebrews 11:31),** Ruth **(Ruth 1–4),** Bathsheba **(2 Samuel 11:2–12:25).**

4. Study the life of Herod the Great. Use a Bible dictionary. Herod is the first recorded enemy of the Kingdom.

*Herod - mom Jew*
*(an Idumean) appointed king of Judea*
*by Roman Senate in 40 BC, gained*
*control in 37 BC to 4 BC - cruel, ruthless*
*ruler - reign noted for splendor -*
*began rebuilding of temple in 20 BC,*
*finished 68 yrs after his death -*
*succeeded by son, Archelaus*

# Lesson 2

# The Change
# (Matthew 3–4)

## Approaching This Study

**Key verse:** "From that time on Jesus began to preach, 'Repent, for the kingdom of heaven is near' " **(Matthew 4:17).**

**Aims of this lesson:** To see ourselves in daily need of repentance; to trust firmly in the forgiveness of our sins, paid for by Jesus Christ; and to respond by bearing the fruit of faith.

## We Need to Change

*A pagan bandit who had become ill was nursed back to health in a Christian hospital. Grateful for the care that was given to him during his illness, he resolved that from then on he would not rob Christians.*

*During his stay in the hospital, he had noted that Christians knew the Ten Commandments and the Apostles' Creed by heart. So each time he was about to commit a robbery, he demanded that the victims recite the Ten Commandments and the Apostles' Creed. If they could do what he demanded, they would not be robbed. If, however, they did not know the Commandments and the Creed from memory, they would be robbed. The whole community quickly responded by memorizing the Command-ments and the Creed. The bandit was soon out of business.*

1. Were the bandit and the entire community moved to repentance and faith? Were they really different than before?

No – both the community + the bandit adapted for their own reasons

---

12

We cannot belong to the kingdom of heaven as we are. We are not acceptable; we cannot fulfill the requirements for citizenship in the Kingdom: "Be holy because I, the Lord your God, am holy" **(Leviticus 19:2)**. "There is not a righteous man on earth who does what is right and never sins" **(Ecclesiastes 7:20).**

A little improvement is not enough. To belong to the kingdom of heaven requires a complete change. The Greek word for repentance used by Jesus and John the Baptist in the chapters of this lesson means to turn around; to reverse one's direction, purpose, and life.

2. Is it possible then for us to belong to the kingdom of heaven and receive the blessings of this kingdom? If so, how?

*Yes.*

# Working with the Text

## Preparing the Way

*announced coming of the Messiah*

Read **Matthew 3:1–12.**

1. Who was John the Baptizer? (Also see **Luke 1:13, 76–80.**)

*Son of Zechariah + Elizabeth
Prophet of Most High
Grew up in Desert of Judea
Began preaching + ministry
when he was ± 30*

2. List several ways in which John's lifestyle was unique **(3:1, 4).**

*preached in Desert of Judea;
preached repentance; dressed
simply in clothes of camel's hair +
a leather belt; ate insects
(locusts were "clean" food) + wild
honey*

Matthew connected the fulfillment of the prophecy of Isaiah with John the Baptizer. See **Isaiah 40:3–5.** The picture given is the Oriental custom of heralding the coming of, and preparing the way for, royalty in their travels.

3. What was the role of John the Baptizer in the kingdom of heaven? (See **John 1:19–23.**)

*John's role was to preach repentance & announce the coming of the Messiah to people w/d chg their ways & their lives in preparation for the coming*

4. Summarize John's message in one word.

*Repent*

5. Why was a complete change of mind and heart necessary as preparation for the coming of the promised King? (See **Matthew 9:12–13; Luke 1:16–17.**)

*Have to acknowledge & repent our sins before we can be aware of the forgiveness given us thru the Holy Spirit when Christ died for us*

Not only did John the Baptizer tell people to repent of their sins, but he pointed to the coming King and Kingdom as a complete solution to the problem.

6. What would the King do? (See **John 1:29.**)

*Look, the Lamb of God who takes away the sins of the world*

7. What was the solution suggested by Peter on the day of Pentecost to those who were troubled by their sins? (See **Acts 2:37–39.**)

*Repent + be baptized, every one of you, in the name of Jesus Christ for the forgiveness of your sins. And you will receive the gift of the Holy Spirit.*

8. What is the result of repentance of sin and faith in Jesus Christ **(3:8)?**

*Produce fruit in keeping w/ repentance*

9. In **Luke 3:10–14** John gave directions to people who repented, believed, and asked, "What should we do?" What would be the fruit of their faith?

*Man w/ 2 tunics, share; man w/food, share; tax collectors, don't collect extra; soldiers, don't extort $ + don't accuse falsely*

10. Webster defines hypocrisy as "the act of playing a part on stage" or "feigning to be what one is not or to believe what one does not." How did John separate the sincere from the pretenders **(3:7–10)?**

*Believers produce fruit in keeping w/ repentance*

11. Baptisms or washings were very much a part of the Old Covenant. See **Genesis 35:2; Exodus 19:10; Numbers 19:7.** What was the purpose of John's baptism **(v. 11a)?** (Also see **Mark 1:4; Luke 3:3.**)

*Baptism of Repentance*

12. What testimony did John give about the promised King and His work?

**Verse 11b—**

*But after me will come one who is more powerful than I, whose sandals I am not fit to carry*

**Verse 11c** (Also see **Acts 2:1–4.**)—

*He will baptize you w/ the Holy Spirit + w/ fire (Pentecost prophecy)*

**Verse 12** (Also see **Psalm 1:4; 96:13.**)—

*He will come to judge everyone + separate the believers from the non-believers.*

## The Baptized King

Read **Matthew 3:13–17.**

Both John the Baptizer and Jesus were about 30 years old at this time. The Law required that priests and teachers be 30 years old before they assumed their special duties. (See **Numbers 4:2–3.**)

1. What did Jesus request of John **(v. 13)**?

*Jesus asked John to baptize Him.*

2. How did John respond to this request **(v. 14)**?

*John tried to deter him saying, "I need to be baptized by you, & do you come to me?"*

3. Why did Jesus insist upon being baptized **(v. 15)**?

*Jesus' baptism fulfilled all righteousness indicating that he was consecrated to God & approved by Him    4 Reasons in footnotes*

## The King Is Tempted

Read **Matthew 4:1–11.**

1. Why was Jesus led by the Spirit into the desert?

*Jesus was led by the Spirit into the desert to be tempted by the devil*

2. What tactics did Satan use?

*Jesus fasted 40 days & nights – devil turn stones to bread; devil throw yourself down from temple – God's care; devil all things – dominion & splendor*

3. How did Jesus overcome Satan's attacks?

*Jesus responded by quoting God's word.*

## The King Begins His Ministry

Read **Matthew 4:12–17.**

1. After the voice of John was silenced by imprisonment, where then did Jesus concentrate His labors?

*Jesus returned to Galilee. Peter's house in Capernaum became Jesus' base of operations during his ministry in Galilee*

The land where the tribes Zebulun and Naphtali formerly had their homes was a land of mixed population, Jews and Gentiles. To Jewish eyes, the proper place for the Messiah's work was Judea, especially Jerusalem. But Isaiah had foretold Jesus' ministry in this place over 700 years before.

2. What message did Jesus preach?

*Jesus preached the same message at John — Repent, for the kingdom of heaven is near.*

## The King Calls and Heals

Read **Matthew 4:18–25.**

1. What did Jesus mean when He said, "I will make you fishers of men"?

*Jesus wld teach them so they cld spread the good news of salvation — catching people to become believers*

2. What three things did Jesus do in His public ministry?

*Jesus taught in the synagogues, preached the good news of the kingdom, + healed every disease + sickness among the people.*

# Applying the Message

1. In what areas of my life would I like to be different?

*patience, strength in my faith, remember who's in chg*

---

2. How do I react when my sin is exposed? (Could it be that the sermon I like the least is the one I need the most?)

*Ashamed, defensive*

3. How can I recognize sin in myself? How does the moral law, the Ten Commandments **(Exodus 20),** help me to see myself as I really am?

*If I remember & review the Ten Commandments, I will KNOW my sins.*

4. Why can I take no credit for my faith in Jesus Christ as my King and Savior **(1 Corinthians 12:3)?**

*My faith has come to me from the Holy Spirit freely & not by anything I've done*

5. What fruit of repentance would I like to see in my life?

*More awareness to I don't keep screwing up the same way over & over again*

6. John the Baptizer minced no words in condemning hypocrisy. Am I in danger of being a make-believer in some area of my life? Explain.

7. For what reasons should I know the Scriptures well? What steps can I take to know God's Word better?

*If I am well versed in Scripture, I will know what the Lord expects of me & why — my faith will be enhanced. READ STUDY*

8. Sorrow over sin is a requirement for faith and the fruit of this faith is good works. When John the Baptizer was preparing the hearts of people for the coming of the promised King, the Lamb of God who takes away the sin of the world, he preached repentance; and that included sorrow over sin, faith in the forgiveness of sins through Christ, and a changed life. How is Christian repentance to be a daily occurrence in my life?

_Every day I sin b/c I am not perfect + .:, every day I need to reflect & repent_

# Taking the Lesson Home

1. Choose one or several important passages from **Matthew 3–4** and memorize them.

2. Study these passages, noting the people who repented and the changes in their lives: **2 Samuel 12:1–15; Luke 15:11–24; 19:1–10; Acts 16:19–34.**

3. Study the life of John the Baptizer by looking at the following passages: **Luke 1:5–80; John 1:6–8, 19–42; Matthew 11:2–19; Mark 6:14–29.**

# Lesson 3

# Blessedness
# (Matthew 5–7)

## Approaching This Study

**Key verse:** "Blessed are the poor in spirit, for theirs is the kingdom of heaven" **(Matthew 5:3).**

**Aim of this lesson:** To affirm that membership in the kingdom of heaven through faith in Jesus Christ brings us daily blessings, and therefore, we can rejoice in all circumstances.

## We Want to Be Happy and Prosperous

*A letter arrived in the mail. It read, "Trust in the Lord with all your heart and He will acknowledge and He will light the way. This prayer has been sent to you for good luck ... You are to receive good luck within four days of receiving this letter ... It must leave you 96 hours after you receive it ... You must make 20 copies of this letter and send it on to your friends, parents, and relatives. After a few days you will get a surprise ... Darin Mairchild received the chain and, not believing in it, threw it away. Nine days later he died. For no reason should this chain be broken."*

What should be done with the letter?

The U.S. Postmaster General says chain letters are illegal and should be reported. But everybody wants good luck. We all want to be happy, to have success in our undertakings, and to enjoy at least the fruits of our labors, if not a little bit more.

*A young man finally purchased the car of his dreams, an Italian sports car, a Ferrari. Wanting everything to go well with himself and his new car, he went to his minister and asked to have it blessed.*

*"Please bless my Ferrari."*

"I can bless almost anything, son, but what's a Ferrari?" asked the minister.

"Never mind," said the young man. "I'll find someone else to bless it." He sped off down the street to a more up-to-date minister.

"Would you please bless my Ferrari, sir?" he asked.

"Wow! A Ferrari! May I take it for a spin?" And the minister roared off around the block.

"Man, what a car! Now what did you say you wanted me to do?" asked the minister.

"Would you please bless it?" asked the young man.

"What's a blessing?"

Just what is a blessing? The dictionary says a blessing is that which makes happy or prosperous.

The first 11 verses of **Matthew chapter 5** are commonly known as the Beatitudes, expressions of supreme blessedness. Jesus Christ, the promised King, speaks to His disciples, those who by faith in Him have spiritual life and are members of His kingdom. They therefore have all the benefits of this kingdom: its promises, its assurances, its hopes, its certainties, its joys, its peace. The blessings or benefits of this kingdom comprise the abundant life we have as a result of our saving relationship with Jesus Christ. How very fortunate, happy, and blessed we are!

# Working with the Text

## Blessed Are . . .

Read **Matthew 5:1–11.**

## . . . The Poor in Spirit (v. 3)

1. The general opinion of the world is "Blessed are those who are rich, great, and honorable." What is the contrast found in **verse 3?**

2. Who are the poor in spirit? (See **Psalm 51:17.**)

3. What is the difference between being spiritually proud and being spiritually poor? What is the end result? (See **Luke 18:9–14.**)

4. What is meant by the kingdom of heaven? (If you have forgotten, look at Session 1.)

5. How long will we remain poor in spirit? (See **1 John 1:6–10.**)

# . . . Those Who Mourn (v. 4)

1. The world would say, "Blessed are the merry." What is the contrast in **verse 4?**

2. What causes believers to mourn?

3. What was Jesus to do for those who mourn, according to **Isaiah 61:1–3?**

4. What comfort does Jesus promise to those who mourn? (See **2 Corinthians 1:3–5.**)

## ... The Meek (v. 5)

1. What do you think the word *meek* means in **verse 5?**

2. How does the world rate meekness?

3. In what ways did Jesus show meekness? (Also see **1 Peter 2:23–24.** Note that by His meekness we have been saved.)

4. What does **Psalm 37:10–11** contrast with meekness?

5. What is the promise of this Beatitude? What does this promise mean to you?

6. How did Abraham demonstrate meekness in his relationship with his nephew Lot **(Genesis 13:5–9)?** Would you have followed Abraham's example?

7. What examples of meekness are given in **Matthew 5:38–42?**

8. Living the Christian life, however, does not mean we must be "door-mats" under the feet of everybody. See **Matthew 21:12–13** and explain.

9. While "poor in spirit" describes our relationship mainly to God, "meekness" describes our relationship mainly to our fellow human beings. It stems from an inner confidence that we are God's holy children by faith in Jesus Christ. We can safely trust His care and providence in our life. Jesus said of Himself, "I am meek and lowly in heart" **(Matthew 11:29 KJV).** Does meekness mean "weakness" or "power under control"? Why?

# . . . Those Who Hunger and Thirst for Righteousness (v. 6)

1. What is the righteousness that Abraham had? (See **Galatians 3:6–14.**)

2. What did Jesus have to do with Abraham's righteousness and ours?

3. Hunger is one of the strongest human drives. Hungering and thirsting are lifelong. The satisfaction that comes from fulfillment of this drive actually increases the desire. How will being "filled" with Christ's righteousness increase our desire for it day after day?

4. What kind of righteousness is mentioned in **Matthew 5:20?**

5. Why does Jesus call us to live God-pleasing lives? (See **John 15:5.**) List some fruit of a God-pleasing life.

# . . . The Merciful (v. 7)

1. Jesus said, "Be merciful, just as your Father is merciful" **(Luke 6:36).** How does the mercy of God show itself to people? (See **Exodus 34:6–7a.**)

2. Zechariah, filled with the Holy Spirit, prophesied about Jesus in **Luke 1:67–75.** What did God's mercy move Him to do?

3. What were the reasons that Jesus became man, according to **Hebrews 2:17?**

4. How does mercy show itself in the lives of the members of God's kingdom? (See **Luke 10:29–37.**) In what ways will the merciful continue to receive mercy? (See **Hebrews 4:16.**)

# ... The Pure in Heart (v. 8)

1. Jesus spoke about the natural heart of people in **Matthew 15:19.** How did He describe it?

2. How did the prophet Jeremiah describe the heart in **Jeremiah 17:9?**

3. What does God want to do with our hearts, according to **Ezekiel 18:30–32?**

4. How does this "change of heart" take place **(Ezekiel 11:19)?**

5. What work does God's Spirit bring about in the believer's heart? (See **Matthew 22:37–40.**)

6. How will the promise of this Beatitude be completely fulfilled? (See **Revelation 7:15.**)

# . . . The Peacemakers (v. 9)

1. **Matthew 5:9** speaks about peacemakers. What similar thought is expressed about Jesus in **Isaiah 9:6–7?** What kind of kingdom will He, the promised King, have?

2. Why did the angels sing about peace on Bethlehem's fields? (See **Luke 2:10–14.**)

3. Jesus came to bring peace between God and man. How did Paul describe this peace in **2 Corinthians 5:19–20** and **Philippians 4:7?** How are we to be ambassadors of peace?

4. With the peace of God in our hearts, we are to "live at peace with everyone" **(Romans 12:18).** How can we live at peace with everyone? (See **Ephesians 4:31–32.**)

# . . . Those Who Are Persecuted (v. 10)

1. Jesus said that His followers are peacemakers, not troublemakers. But Jesus said to His disciples, "If they persecuted Me, they will persecute you also" **(John 15:20).** What did the prophet Isaiah say would happen to the Messiah? (See **Isaiah 53:3–6.**) Why did He endure persecution?

2. What did Peter say about the suffering of Jesus in **1 Peter 2:21?**

3. The disciples endured persecution for the sake of Jesus and His kingdom. Jesus said that when persecution comes His disciples should rejoice. How can His followers rejoice when persecution comes? Give details from **Acts 5:40–42.**

4. In what different ways can persecution come?

5. Why shouldn't we be afraid of a few "scars" in serving Christ? (See **2 Timothy 4:7–8.**)

The full life, rich and abundant, is the result of the saving work of Jesus Christ. "I have come that they may have life, and have it to the full" **(John 10:10)**. With Jesus as our King, we belong to His kingdom and enjoy all of its blessings.

Read the rest of the Sermon on the Mount in **Matthew 5–7,** noting how this abundant life will show itself in the lives of the believers.

# Applying the Message

1. What is the difference between being "poor in spirit" and struggling with feelings of inferiority? How does being "poor in spirit" increase my feelings of self-worth? What relationship exists between being "poor in spirit" and my attendance at the Lord's Supper?

2. How can I be a channel of Christ's comfort to those who mourn over their sins; to those who mourn over a loss or sorrow; to those who mourn over the death of a loved one?

3. What relationship does Christian meekness have to self-assertiveness training, civil rights, desire for promotions in the business world, political campaigns, and business ethics?

4. The blessing of inheriting the earth refers to material possessions or the physical blessings of this earth. How does this influence my attitude towards conservation, ecology, and stewardship?

5. What steps can I take to increase my spiritual appetite?

6. How do mercy and peacemaking apply to Christian family living? What steps can I take to make my home more blessed?

# Taking the Lesson Home

1. Outline the main thoughts of Christ's Sermon on the Mount. Make suggestions for personal growth with each thought.

2. Review the orders of worship that your congregation uses, noting the use of the word *mercy.*

3. Study the words *salt* and *light* and their applications to the daily life of members of Christ's kingdom.

4. Memorize one or several verses from these three chapters that have special meaning for you now.

# Lesson 4

# Follow the King
# (Matthew 8–10)

## Approaching This Study

**Key verse:** "Anyone who does not take his cross and follow Me is not worthy of Me" **(Matthew 10:38).**

**Aim of this lesson:** To willingly accept our obligations, responsibilities, and crosses as followers of Jesus Christ, who put Himself and His kingdom first in our lives.

## We Need a Purpose for Living

*"We know that we are outnumbered and that the government troops are coming, but we are prepared to fight to the death, if need be, for our cause," said the rebel spokesman.*

That's commitment, binding oneself wholeheartedly to a cause or to a person.

Life without a cause is purposeless and boring. It just doesn't seem worth living.

The greatest cause is the cause of Jesus Christ and His kingdom. This cause demands our allegiance, our loyalty, our enthusiasm, and our commitment. If Jesus is our King and we are members of His kingdom by repentance and faith, then the cause of the kingdom demands first priority in our lives.

Why then is it said by many professing Christians, "Religion is fine as long as God doesn't get in my way"?

Jesus calls us to follow Him. Can we just keep right on doing our own thing, setting our own priorities? Or will following Jesus cause some changes in our lives?

What does it mean to follow Jesus?

# Working with the Text

In **Matthew 8:1–17** Jesus, the promised King, continued His compassionate work, fulfilling the words of **Isaiah 53:4:** "Surely He took up our infirmities and carried our sorrows."

Great crowds followed Him everywhere He went. It was difficult for Him to find time to eat, sleep, or pray. Some followed Him because they wanted the thrill of seeing a miracle, some because they thought He was a great teacher. Some turned to Him for help in desperation, and others followed Him because they believed that He was the Promised One, the Son of God, the Savior who would take away all their sins.

## The Cost of Following the King

Read **Matthew 8:18–22.**

Following Jesus was not a matter to be taken lightly or a decision to be made carelessly or thoughtlessly. One meaning for *follow*, according to the dictionary, is "to move or act under the leadership, control, or authority of" someone. Faith in Jesus is a binding relationship. Among other things, it involves commitment, allegiance, and loyalty.

A man who was educated in the Law and had been qualified to teach by the Jewish authorities offered to follow Jesus.

1. Why did Jesus direct him to count the cost **(v. 20)?** (Also see **Luke 14:28–33.**)

2. According to **1 Timothy 6:17–19,** what attitude are followers of Jesus commanded to adopt toward material comforts?

3. In **Matthew 6:25–33,** what is Jesus' answer to our concerns about our physical needs? With which Beatitude would you connect this promise? (See **Matthew 5:3–11.**)

4. In **Matthew 15:3–6** Jesus corrected the false idea of the Pharisees and teachers of the law that a person didn't need to keep the Fourth Commandment, "Honor your father and mother," if he or she was doing something for God. What is the greatest way of showing concern for a loved one **(Luke 9:60)?**

5. What do these verses teach a follower of Jesus about priorities in his or her life?

# Miracles of the King
Read **Matthew 8:23–9:8.**
The miracles of Jesus pointed people to the fact that He was more than a man, that He was true God. List at least four ways in which Jesus showed that He was true God.

# The King Calls Levi
Read **Matthew 9:9–13.**
Not everyone wanted to follow Jesus **(8:34)** nor did everyone accept Him as true God **(9:3).** But Matthew did.

1. Who was Matthew? (Also see **Mark 2:14.**)

*Matthew* means "gift of the Lord" and may have been the name given to Levi when He became a follower of Jesus.

2. What was Matthew's occupation?

The Roman system of taxation worked this way: The tax was assessed for a certain region. Wealthy Roman citizens paid the assessed taxes from money they collected from the local people. For these Romans, it was an investment. If more than the assessed amount could be collected, they received a profit on their investment. These wealthy people did not do the actual collecting. Chief publicans or tax collectors were placed in charge of collecting taxes in different areas. Zacchaeus was such a chief collector. Under the chief collector were common collectors, like Matthew, who received the taxes from the local people. At every level, there was opportunity for graft. Tax collectors or publicans were hated by the Jews because they served the Romans and because they collected excessively to make themselves rich.

Matthew was a customs officer at Capernaum on the great caravan route that came in from Damascus and the East. In order to hold that position, he had to know Greek and to be well educated.

3. What was Matthew's immediate response to Jesus' call, "Follow Me"?

Matthew must have been a believer in Jesus, the promised King, before this time. Many of Jesus' miracles were performed in Capernaum **(Matthew 11:23).** This was a call for Matthew to do a special work and to live in a special relationship with Jesus.

4. How do you think Matthew's lifestyle was changed after he accepted Jesus' call?

5. Matthew then hosted a celebration in honor of Jesus. How is the dinner party described in **Luke 5:29?** Why do you think Matthew invited tax collectors and "sinners" to his party?

6. The Pharisees would not be present in such company. They stood outside, watched the partygoers, and criticized them. What question did they ask Jesus' disciples? What was Jesus' response to their question? Who are the sick? Who are the healthy who don't need a doctor? (Also see **Revelation 3:17.**)

7. How does Jesus' direction to the Pharisees in **9:13** show that He was concerned for their souls too? Where would they have to go to find the answer? (Also see **Hosea 6:6.**)

8. How does **9:13** direct us to the blessings of following the King and of belonging to His kingdom as found in **Matthew 5:7?** (Also see Session 3.)

## The King Teaches about Fasting
Read **Matthew 9:14–17.**

Jesus connected fasting and mourning. His followers were not mourning but rejoicing. Being a follower of Jesus is cause for rejoicing. Though we live our lives in a real world filled with sin and trouble and death, we can "rejoice in the Lord always" **(Philippians 4:4).**

1. What two examples from daily living did Jesus use to describe what it means to be a follower of His and a member of His kingdom **(9:16–17)?**

2. Why is everything new for a follower of Jesus? (See **John 3:3; 2 Corinthians 5:17; 1 Peter 1:3.**)

## More Miracles by the King

Read **Matthew 9:18–38.**

Jesus the King continued His work of teaching, preaching the Good News of the Kingdom, and healing.

1. What was Jesus' attitude toward the crowds of people who flocked to Him **(v. 36)?**

2. What did He tell His followers to do **(v. 38)?**

## The King Sends Out His Followers

Read **Matthew 10:1–15.**

Although He had many followers, Jesus picked twelve for a special relationship with Him and a special work. (See **Acts 10:42.**) They were called *apostles*, which means "messengers, ambassadors, sent ones."

1. List the twelve apostles, noting the brothers and other ways of identifying them. (Also see **Mark 3:16–19; Luke 6:14–16.**)

2. When Jesus sent out the Twelve, what orders were they given? On whose authority were they to do these things **(10:1)?**

## The King Assigns a Task

Read **Matthew 10:16–33.**

Sharing the Good News of the Kingdom is a blessed task with blessed results in the minds and lives of those who believe the message. But there will always be those who reject it, who are enemies of the Kingdom.

1. What will the enemies of the Kingdom do?

2. How are the followers of Jesus to react to these tactics of the enemy **(vv. 16, 19–20, 22–23)?**

3. Why can we as followers of Jesus expect opposition **(vv. 24–25)?**

4. Fear often paralyzes us, keeping us from doing what we should. Also, fear may spur us to wrong action. How do followers of Jesus handle their fears **(vv. 26–33)?**

## The King . . . First in Our Lives

Read **Matthew 10:34–42.**

The King must be number one in our lives if we are His followers and members of His kingdom. Even though Jesus admonishes us to love our families **(Ephesians 5:25** and **Titus 2:4),** He is to be loved most of all.

1. What does it mean to be worthy of Jesus?

2. Let us remember that there is no cross without Christ. The cross signifies those hurts that come to us because we confess and live for Jesus. How can a person lose his or her life and yet find it?

3. Jesus promised to reward His faithful followers, though we have not deserved or earned that reward. What different kinds of reward did Jesus speak of in **verses 40–42?**

4. What does **Matthew 5:12** have to say about reward for crossbearing?

# Applying the Message

1. What are some of the "costs" I encounter as I follow Jesus and share the "free" gift of the Gospel? Have I ever backed away from an opportunity because the costs were too great? What actions can I take to evaluate opportunities and to have the courage to follow?

2. Where do "material comforts" rate in my list of priorities? How does this affect my giving for the Lord?

3. What obligation does a forgiven sinner have to other sinners? For what person (or people) do I have a special concern? What action can I take to share the Good News of the Kingdom with that person (or those people)?

4. How can I show concern for sinners without condoning their sin?

5. How does knowing Jesus' compassion personally help me to face difficult situations in my life?

6. How do the miracles of Jesus in these chapters encourage me to follow Jesus?

# Taking the Lesson Home

1. Study the lives of the twelve apostles.
2. Make a prayer list for Kingdom concerns. Write a prayer for each and share with the group both your plans for prayer times and some of your prayers.
3. Read one of the many available books about modern martyrs.
4. Select one or more promises of God that strengthen you especially as you follow Jesus. Commit them to memory.

# Lesson 5

# Listen to the King
# (Matthew 11–13)

## Approaching This Study

**Key verse:** "He who has ears, let him hear" **(Matthew 11:15).**

**Aim of this lesson:** To learn to listen carefully to God's Word so that by the power of the Spirit we may understand with our minds, believe with our hearts, and act accordingly in our lives.

## We Need to Listen

*It had been a perfect vacation at the lake. But the time had come to pack up and return home. Each member of the family had a job to do except Joey. He was the youngest, and he could play outside until the family was ready to leave.*

*Everyone was busy. Suddenly there was a banging on the door, and Joey screamed, "Help me! Help me! Will somebody please open the door?" But no one went to the door. No one paid much attention. The packing must be done quickly. The screams and the banging continued, then became less, and finally stopped.*

*When someone opened the door to carry a load to the car, there lay Joey on the porch. He had fallen on a broken bottle, cut an artery, and was bleeding.*

*No one had really listened.*

Why does Jesus, the promised King, say again and again, "If you have ears, listen!"

Why did the Lord say by the mouth of His prophet, "Son of man, you are living among a rebellious people. They have eyes to see but do not see and ears to hear but do not hear" **(Ezekiel 12:2)**?

There must be more to listening than just hearing words or sounds!

# Working with the Text

## The King's Servant

Read **Matthew 11:1–15.**

1. What question did John the Baptizer's followers ask of Jesus **(v. 3)**?

2. How did Jesus direct them to listen to what God had told them in the Scriptures **(vv. 4–5)**? (Also see **Isaiah 26:19; 29:18–24; 35:5–6; 61:1–2; Luke 4:16–21.**)

3. If the followers of John listened to the Lord speaking in the Scriptures and compared the teaching and the works of Jesus with the prophecies of Isaiah, what conclusion would they draw? What would result?

## To Listen and to Understand

Read **Matthew 11:16–30.**

God's complaint with some of His chosen people under the Old Covenant was that their ears were stopped up and they would not listen to Him. Their eyes were blind and they would not recognize His work. Jesus encountered the same reaction when He walked on this earth.

1. What characteristic is necessary if a person is to listen and understand **(v. 25)**? (Also see **Matthew 5:3–6; 18:3; Mark 10:15.**)

2. Worldly or human knowledge is acquired by study, observation, experimentation, practice, etc., and is constantly changing. How is spiritual knowledge and understanding achieved **(vv. 25–27)? Matthew 5:8** speaks about seeing God. How can a person get to know God the Father better **(v. 27)?**

3. What special message does Jesus want people to hear **(vv. 28–30)?**

4. What does Jesus want to give to His followers?

5. What does He want His followers to do?

## The King of the Sabbath

Read **Matthew 12:1–21.**

1. When Jesus was criticized, He directed His opponents to the Scriptures. If they would listen and understand what God was saying in the Scriptures, they would not misunderstand Jesus, His teaching, and His works. How did the Pharisees respond to Jesus' teaching?

2. For those who did hear, Jesus fulfilled the prophecy of **Isaiah 42:1–4.** How does this prophecy describe the promised King? How did He do the work of the Kingdom?

# The King and His Foe

Read **Matthew 12:22–50.**

1. A person cannot stay neutral to the call of the King and the kingdom of heaven. Just as some called Jesus "the Son of David," the Promised One, others called Him a son of the devil. If we confess that Jesus is the promised King and our Savior, who gets the credit for this confession? (See **Matthew 16:17; 1 Corinthians 12:3.**)

2. To those who rejected Jesus and kept demanding proof that Jesus really was the promised King, Jesus said they would only get one sign, the sign of the prophet Jonah. What is the sign of the prophet Jonah **(12:39–40; Jonah 1:17)?**

3. What blessing is received by those who listen and believe that Jesus is the promised King and their Savior **(v. 50)?**

# The King Uses Parables to Teach

Read **Matthew 13:1–17.**

**Matthew 13** is sometimes called the Parable Chapter.

A little girl once defined a parable as an "earthly story with a heavenly meaning." Jesus, the Master Teacher, took stories and pictures from everyday life to reveal and teach spiritual truths to the believers.

These points are helpful for the correct understanding of parables:

1. Each parable has some picture from nature or life that we must first understand.

2. Each parable teaches a spiritual truth that must be discovered. Jesus explained several parables. Other parables must be explained in their context, or the setting in which they were taught.

3. Each parable has a "point of comparison." We must ask the question,

"What two things are being compared?"

4. Not all details in a parable have to be explained. Some details are there just to flesh out the story, not to make a point. Whenever we interpret parabes and their details, we dare never draw lessons that contradict the plain teachings of God's Word.

## Parable of the Sower (vv. 3–23)

1. Why did Jesus speak in parables **(vv. 11–17)?**

2. Describe in your own words the "earthly picture" in **verses 1–8.** Remember that the sower did not have modern machinery and that the seed was all sown by hand. Notice the four different types of soil.

3. What is the seed **(v. 19)?** (Also see **Luke 8:11.**)

4. Who then is the sower?

5. How does He continue sowing the Word? (See **Luke 10:16.**)

6. List the unique qualities of this Word given in **Psalm 119:103–105; Romans 1:16; 2 Timothy 3:16** and **1 Peter 1:23–25.**

7. What is one of the marks of discipleship found in **John 8:31–32?**

8. Jesus described four different kinds of hearers by comparing them with four different kinds of soil. How did Jesus describe the first kind of hearer **(v. 19)?** (Also see **Luke 8:12.**)

9. How does Jesus describe the second kind of hearer, who is like the seed sown on rocky ground **(vv. 20–21)? John 6:60–66** reports that some disciples stopped following Jesus. Why? What are some of the ways in which tribulation and persecution come to the followers of Christ? (See **Matthew 10:22, 24–25; 24:9–13.**)

10. How did Jesus describe the third kind of hearer, who is like the thorny soil **(v. 22)?** (Also see **Luke 8:14.**)

11. What is the fourth kind of hearer, whom Jesus compares to good soil **(v. 23)?** What did Jesus call people who hear and keep His Word **(Luke**

**11:28)?** What purpose do believers have for living? What is their motive for fruitbearing **(2 Corinthians 5:14–15)?**

12. In **John 15:1–6,** Jesus said the Father looks for fruit in the lives of His children. Jesus also said that unless we are attached to Him by faith, it is impossible to bear fruit in our lives. List the fruit of faith found in **John 15:7–12.**

## Other Parables of the King

Read **Matthew 13:24–52.**

The parables recorded in this section speak about the nature, value, size, and growth of the Kingdom. Three times in these chapters (**11:15; 13:9;** and **13:43**) Jesus spoke the words, "He who has ears, let him hear." State in your own words what Jesus meant.

## A King without Honor

Read **Matthew 13:53–58.**

How did the unbelief of people in Jesus' own country affect His ministry?

# Applying the Message

1. What are the causes of spiritual deafness? Do I have any of the symptoms? If so, what are they?

2. Communication involves both speaking and listening. Jesus can talk to me, He can reach my heart, in many different ways. List ways in which the seed of the Word can be sown in my heart. In which of these ways is Jesus speaking through me to others?

3. What would be a good prayer for me to use when I begin the study of God's Word? (See **1 Samuel 3:10.**)

4. What tactics does Satan use to keep the Word from taking root and growing in worship services? in church organizations? in my personal spiritual life?

5. The worst weeds or thorns in my life are _____. How can I weed them out?

6. How can I bear more fruit—thirty-, sixty-, a hundred-fold—in the following areas of my life: worship, Bible study, Christian giving, home and family relationships, stewardship of time?

# Taking the Lesson Home

1. List the ways in which Jesus, His words, and His kingdom were rejected in these chapters.

2. Study and explain the other parables in **Matthew 13**, following the suggestions given in this lesson.

3. Select one or several important passages from this lesson and memorize them.

# Lesson 6

# Faith in the King
# (Matthew 14–18:14)

## Approaching This Study

**Key verse:** "I tell you the truth, unless you change and become like little children, you will never enter the kingdom of heaven" **(Matthew 18:3).**

**Aim of this lesson:** To grow stronger in our faith as we overcome doubt and follow Jesus.

## We Want to Believe

*Everyone in the house walked with a quiet step and spoke softly. There were no smiles. The mother of the family lay critically ill.*

*But in the backyard, two little children played happily and noisily.*

*An adult came out of the house and said to the children, "How can you play and make so much noise? Don't you know that your mother is very sick and might die?"*

*The children answered, "But we prayed to Jesus. He is taking care of Mommy."*

Would you like to have such complete confidence in Jesus?

Life is hard to face. Troubles, problems, sickness, and death are all around us. Life is not a bed of roses. Even those who are members of the kingdom of heaven through faith in Jesus Christ as the promised King and Savior experience troubles. We know that our sins are forgiven but how do we cope with day-to-day problems?

Jesus says in **John 16:33,** "In this world you will have trouble. But take heart! I have overcome the world." Jesus, the promised King, says that He has won the victory over the world and its tribulations. We, as members of His kingdom, share that victory.

But how do we share Jesus' victory over the world and its troubles? **1 John 5:4** says, "This is the victory that has overcome the world, even our faith."

Many people claim to have faith. They have faith in themselves, in another person such as a government leader or a doctor, in a program or system. Faith cannot stand alone. It must be built on something. Faith always requires an object to which it clings and in which it trusts.

But misplaced confidence is a false faith. Sincerity is not enough. A sincere person can get up at night and in the dark take a spoonful from a bottle marked "Arsenic," believing that it is medicine to relieve a sickness. But that sincere person would still be poisoned.

Faith must be built upon the right foundation. The promises of God and the faith of Christians dovetail with each other. **Romans 4:3** and **Genesis 15:6** tell us that Abraham's faith was founded on what God said to him. Abraham believed that God spoke the truth and that what God promised would happen, even though he had to wait patiently for it.

**Hebrews 11:1** defines faith as "being sure of what we hope for and certain of what we do not see." To believe is to be certain of things we have not seen, as though we actually saw them.

We want such a victorious faith. We ask for it in the prayer of the troubled father, "I do believe; help me overcome my unbelief!" **(Mark 9:24).**

# Working with the Text

## The Cost of Following the King

Read **Matthew 14:1–12.**

John the Baptizer, the herald of the promised King and the Kingdom, was killed because he voiced his faith courageously.

## The King Feeds 5,000 Hungry Subjects

Read **Matthew 14:13–21.**

1. What were the circumstances when this great crowd of people sought help from Jesus **(vv. 13–14)?** *John the Baptist had been beheaded; Jesus went alone by boat to a solitary place; the people went by foot to follow him; he felt compassion*

2. What was the concern of the disciples that evening **(v. 15)?** *The place they went to was remote; it was getting towards evening; they had no food with them*

3. What resources did they have to solve the problem **(vv. 16–17)**? (Also see **John 6:8–9.**)

*Jesus said the crowds do not need to leave for food; the disciples said we have only 5 loaves of bread + 2 fish.*

4. Jesus gave instructions for an orderly meal **(v. 19)**. Then He took their meager resources, a boy-sized lunch, and spoke the table prayer. After He had broken the lunch into pieces, the disciples began to pass around the food. How much did each person eat? What was the amount of leftovers? How many people were served **(v. 20–21)**? (Also see **John 6:11–13.**)

*Each person ate until they were satisfied (5,000 mem, besides womem + childrem). There were 12 basketfuls of brokem pieces left over.*

# The King Walks on Water

Read **Matthew 14:22–36.**

This crowd that had been miraculously fed had a misplaced confidence or faith. See **John 6:14–15.** They wanted Jesus to be their earthly king, their bread king. Jesus then ordered His disciples to go by boat to Capernaum on the other side of the Sea of Galilee while He sent the crowd of people back to their homes.

1. What happened to these seasoned seamen as they rowed across the lake **(14:24)**?

*When the boat was a considerable distance from shore it was buffeted by waves b/c of high winds*

The Sea of Galilee, located between high ridges, is noted for the fury of the sudden storms that sweep over it.

Between 3 a.m. and 6 a.m., the fourth watch of the night, the disciples were still in the middle of the lake. Jesus came to them, walking on the water.

2. How did the disciples react to the sight of Jesus **(v. 26)**?

*terrified; The disciples were; they thought they were seeing a ghost.*

3. How did Peter demonstrate his faith (vv. 28–29)?

*Peter asked the Lord to "tell me to come to you on the water"*

4. What caused Peter to sink (vv. 30–31)?

*When Peter felt the wind he became afraid, lost his faith & doubted Jesus wld see to his safety so began to sink*

5. Besides walking on the water Himself and enabling Peter to walk on the water, what other miracles did Jesus perform at this time (v. 32)? (Also see **John 6:21**.)

*The wind died down when Jesus & Peter got into the boat; they reached the shore of Gennesaret safely*

6. How did the disciples respond to these miracles (v. 33)?

*Their belief was strengthened & they said "Truly you are the Son of God"*

## The King Teaches about Clean and Unclean

Read **Matthew 15:1–20.**

The Pharisees and teachers of the law had faith in the tradition of the elders. What did they reject?

*They rejected God's law & instead adhered strictly to the laws & traditions handed down orally from Moses*

## The King of All People

Read **Matthew 15:21–39.**

When Jesus traveled to the Gentile territory of Tyre and Sidon, north of Galilee, many there had already learned about Him.

1. What was the request of the Gentile woman, identified in the gospels by both the old name of her country, Canaan, and the current name, Syrian

Phoenicia **(v. 22)**?

*She asked Jesus to heal her daughter from demon possession*

2. What do her words indicate about her knowledge of Jesus?

*She called Jesus "Lord, Son of David" + she asked him to have mercy on her*

3. Tested by silence and by Jesus' words to His disciples that His work at this time was among the Jews, what did this woman do **(v. 25)**?

*She continued to plead to Jesus. She knelt before him saying "Lord, help me".*

4. The Jews called the Gentiles "dogs," meaning people who were outsiders and unclean. When Jesus finally spoke to the woman, He didn't speak of stray dogs but of pet house dogs. How was the faith of this Gentile woman strengthened by that remark **(vv. 26–27)**?

*children's bread → lost sheep of Israel. She was gentile so it gospel first given to Jews, the wld still [?] for "crumbs"*

Merely knowing facts to be true is not faith. However, if these facts mean something to you personally and if you feel sure that they will benefit you, then you have faith in them.

5. What were the results of this woman's persistence **(v. 28)**? Why?

*Her faith was rewarded. Jesus healed her daughter*

## The King Is Challenged by His Critics

### Read **Matthew 16:1–12.**

Just as the secrets of the kingdom of heaven taught by Jesus in parables cannot be understood without faith, so the unbelieving Pharisees and Sadducees could not understand the signs or miracles Jesus performed **(vv. 1–4)**.

What does the disciples' misunderstanding of Jesus' words indicate about their faith (vv. 5–12)?

*Thier faith was not strong + unquestioning enuf to completely put thier trust in Jesus*

## Who Is This King?

Read **Matthew 16:13–28.**

1. The question "Who is Jesus Christ?" is an important one. How did many people respond to that question (v. 14)? (Also see 14:2.)

*"Some say John the Baptist; others say Elijah; + others Jeremiah or one of the prophets"*

2. How did Peter, as the spokesman for all the disciples, respond to that question (16:16)?

*You are the Christ, the Son of the living God*

3. What does Peter's confession that Jesus is the Christ, the Son of the living God mean? (See **John 1:32–34, 41, 45, 49.**)

*Peter believed by faith*

4. What is the rock upon which Jesus will build His church (v. 18)? (Also see **1 Corinthians 3:11; Ephesians 2:20.**)

*Peter's faith is the foundation on which the church is built (= Jesus + the teachings of the apostles + prophets)*

The kingdom of heaven is entered only by faith in Jesus Christ as the Savior who forgives sins. Unbelief closes the door to the kingdom of heaven (v. 19).

5. Since the Jews who did not believe still looked for an earthly king or messiah, Jesus told His disciples not to tell others that He was the Christ (v. 20). But He began to tell them specifically what His work would be. What specifics did Jesus give His disciples (v. 21)? How did Peter react to

Jesus' words **(v. 22)**? Why did Jesus call Peter "Satan" **(v. 23)**? Which temptation of Satan in **Matthew 4** was Peter repeating?

*Jesus wld go to Jerusalem, suffer many things, be killed, & on 3rd day rise to life. Peter rebuked Jesus b/c he cldn't believe it wld happen. Jesus was treating Peter as an adversary.*

Faith in Jesus Christ as Savior includes the cross. Jesus took the punishment for the sins of all people by His suffering and death. His resurrection proved that God the Father accepted His sacrifice on behalf of everyone. Now through His cross we have life. Our faith brings us all the blessings of the kingdom of heaven. But we must face the opposition of the enemies of the Kingdom just as Christ did.

## The King Is Revealed

Read **Matthew 17:1–13.**

The transfiguration of Christ demonstrates what Peter confessed: Jesus, the man born of the Virgin Mary, is the Christ, the Son of the living God.

## The King's Power over Demons

Read **Matthew 17:14–21.**

1. What was the affliction of the son whose father brought him to Jesus **(v. 15)**?

*He suffered from seizures & demon possessed*

2. In **Matthew 10:8,** Jesus gave His disciples His authority to drive out demons. Why then couldn't they cure the afflicted boy **(17:20)**?

*The disciples had too little faith to have the power given to them to heal*

Faith has a double function. First, it clings to the promise of God and appropriates to itself what this promise offers, namely, the grace of God and the merits of Christ. This is the justifying and saving power of faith. Both the person with weak faith and the person with strong faith trust in the same promise. And both believers receive the same grace and forgiveness.

The second function of faith is its sanctifying power. It produces fruit or good works in the life of believers.

Jesus' answer did not refer to redeeming or justifying faith such as Peter had confessed in **Matthew 16:16,** but to the disciples' lack of a firm reliance on God's power and promises.

3. What is included in the "mustard seed" picture of faith **(17:20; 13:31–32)?** The father said to Jesus, "I do believe; help me overcome my unbelief!" **(Mark 9:24).** How can faith grow and increase? (See **Romans 10:17; Colossians 3:16.)**

# The King Teaches of His Kingdom

Read **Matthew 18:1–14.**

1. Why is it necessary for people to become like children in order to enter the kingdom of heaven?

*trusting + humble → faith to rely on Jesus to take care of us*

2. How do people who are "poor in spirit" and "meek" indicate a child-like" response **(Matthew 5:3, 5)?** (Also see Session 3.)

3. How did Jesus direct Nicodemus to a childlike faith **(John 3:1–16)?** What must a person lay aside in order to have a childlike faith? (See **Romans 3:20; 1 Corinthians 1:21.)**

4. God the Father wants faith to grow. Jesus, the promised King, will do everything necessary to strengthen a weak faith **(Matthew 12:20).** What

concern did Jesus show for the little children who believed in Him **(18:5–6)?**

5. What concern is shown in **Romans 14:20–21** and **Romans 15:1–2** for those who are weak in faith?

6. How serious is the matter of leading a child or any person astray **(18:7–14)?**

7. Why does a childlike faith result in greatness in the kingdom of heaven **(vv. 1, 4)?**

# Applying the Message

1. What promises of God are especially precious to me as I face the troubles of life? How can I show my trust in these promises?

2. What doubts have troubled me in the past? How did Jesus grant me victory over those doubts? How can I help others who are troubled by doubts?

3. What example does the Gentile Woman's persistence give me for prayer?

4. According to **John 3:16,** what is necessary for me to enter and remain in the kingdom of God? What promise is made to me?

5. Christian hope is basically faith concerning things to come. It is founded on God's promises in His Word. How can I follow **1 Peter 3:15,** confessing my faith with gentleness and respect?

6. How would I reply to the statement, "It doesn't matter what you believe as long as you are sincere"?

# Taking the Lesson Home

1. Look at these passages: **Luke 8:13–14; John 5:44; 2 Corinthians 10:5; 1 Timothy 1:18–19; 6:20–21; 2 Peter 2:20–21; 1 John 2:15.** Discover some of the reasons why people lose their faith.

2. Study the symbols for faith used in the Bible and in Christian art.

3. Study the faith chapter of the Bible, **Hebrews 11.**

4. Study some Christian hymns that speak about faith.

5. Memorize one or more promises of God that you wish to trust more every day.

# Lesson 7

# Forgive as the King Forgives (Matthew 18:15–19:15)

## Approaching This Study

**Key verses:** " 'Lord, how many times shall I forgive my brother when he sins against me? Up to seven times?' Jesus answered, 'I tell you, not seven times, but seventy-seven times' " **(Matthew 18:21–22).**

**Aim of this lesson:** To learn to forgive others and to show them mercy because God has forgiven us greatly through Christ the King.

## We Need to Forgive

*Some years ago George was selling his farm and machinery at an auction. His sister, Tillie, bought the big tractor, but she didn't have the full amount of cash on hand to pay for it. George asked Tillie not to use the tractor until it was paid for.*

*Tillie was a widow and her son, Charlie, was doing the farmwork for his mother. Before the big tractor was fully paid for, Charlie used it to do the spring plowing.*

*George was so angry at Tillie that he wouldn't speak to her, even after the debt was fully paid. They both attended the same church, but for a long time the brother and the sister did not speak to each other.*

*It took the illness of their mother to break down the barrier between them. They held a grudge for 10 years.*

Why is forgiving so difficult for us?

There are many times in life when someone hurts, offends, or treats us unjustly. We live in a sinful world filled with sinful people. How should we react? How would God have us react toward others, especially toward those who have wronged us? Those are the questions we will consider in this lesson.

# Working with the Text

## Greatest in the Kingdom

Read **Matthew 18:15–20.**

1. Jesus spoke to His disciples about relationships between believers. Note the steps of admonition and church discipline. What should believers do when something breaks down their relationship with another person, especially another believer? (See **Matthew 18:15.**)

*If someone sins against you, go to that person & tell him/her — try to get it reconciled.*

2. Every sin, even though committed against another person, is basically a sin against God. All sin transgresses God's laws. What should be the motive and the spirit of the private confrontation? (See **Galatians 6:1; 1 John 4:19–21.**)

*The motive should be to bring the person to compliance w/ the Lord's commandments for us. Do it in the spirit of love & gentleness*

3. How could the procedure described in **18:16** help both people in a dispute?

*Taking others along will help both sides to stay calm & see the situation as it really happened.*

4. What would be the third step **(v. 17)**?

*Tell it to the church — get the congregation involved to bring the errant person to contrition*
*pagan tax collect*

The purpose of all the steps of admonition is to bring erring Christians to the knowledge of their sins so that they might repent, accept the forgiveness of sin through faith in Jesus Christ, turn from their sin by the power of the Spirit, and become one with God and their fellow believers. If the steps are not successful, such people should still receive special loving care with prayers for their repentance.

5. **Matthew 18:15–20** are words of Jesus directed to individual believers who gather together in congregations. How many believers are needed to form a congregation **(vv. 19–20)?** What does it mean to be gathered in Jesus' name?

*whenever 2 or 3 are gathered in my name. When believers gather in Jesus' name they fellowship w/one another*

6. What authority or power does Jesus give to the believers **(v. 18)?** (Also see **Matthew 16:19.**)

*Authority to forgive or not to forgive* *can't forgive i't when there no repentance*

7. What opens the door to the kingdom of heaven? (See **Matthew 9:2; John 20:31.**) What closes the door to the kingdom of heaven? (See **John 3:18.**)

*faith & belief in Jesus* *disbelief in God's son — lack of faith*

## The King Teaches More about Forgiveness

Read **Matthew 18:21–35.**

Peter got the message that forgiveness was to be an essential part of the believer's life. Jewish tradition said that forgiving a person three times for the same offense was enough.

1. What does Jesus' answer to Peter's question teach believers, members of His kingdom, about forgiveness?

*We should continue to forgive sincere sinners just as we are continually forgiven*

2. To illustrate the point, Jesus told a parable to Peter and the other disciples. Remember that a parable is an earthly story with a heavenly meaning.

The king in the earthly story was an oriental monarch with absolute power over the lives and property of his subjects. His servants were high government officials, responsible to the king for collecting revenues.

What was the predicament of one servant who had accumulated a huge debt, estimated at millions of dollars? Why was the king's mercy the servant's only hope?

*The debt was such a lg am't there was no way he cld pay it. The king cld have sold the servant, wife & children into slavery & sold all his possessions*

3. How did that same servant treat a fellow servant who owed him a relatively small debt, 100 days' pay? What did the action of the forgiven servant towards his fellow servant reveal about his heart?

*He grabbed him & began to choke; he ignored his plea & put him into prison. He had a black heart; he wasn't comtrite*

4. What happened when the king heard about the action of the forgiven servant?

*The king turned the servants over to the jailers to be tortured until the lg debt was pd.*

5. What is the heavenly meaning given in **verse 35?**

*If forgiveness doesn't come from our heart, then God will treat us just as harshly as the king treated the servant - can't just go thru motions*

6. What is the debt we owe God the Father? (See **Matthew 6:12; Romans 6:23.**) Why can we never repay this debt? (See **Isaiah 64:6; Romans 3:20; Galatians 3:10.**) How does God the Father show mercy to us? (See **Isaiah 43:25; Matthew 9:2; John 1:29; 3:16; Romans 5:11; Colossians 2:13.**) How does God the Father expect us to treat those who owe us debts that are small in comparison? (See **Matthew 6:12; Luke**

**6:36; Ephesians 4:32; Colossians 3:13.**)

*We owe God debt b/c of our sinfulness. We can't repay debt b/c we continue to sin. We have been shown mercy thru Jesus' death. We must forgive others*

7. If a person withholds mercy and forgiveness from others, what does that show about his or her attitude towards God's mercy and forgiveness?

*Lack of gratitude; Lapse in faith; Lack of recognition that we don't deserve forgiveness — it has been given to us*

# The King Teaches about Relationships

Read **Matthew 19:1–15.**

Another area where forgiveness is necessary is family living.

The Pharisees thought they had really caught Jesus with a trick question. There were two schools of Jewish thought: Shammai taught that there should be no divorce except for adultery. Hillel taught that a man could get a divorce for many reasons, such as his wife burning the dinner or his finding another woman he liked better.

1. Where does Jesus direct the Pharisees to find the answer to their question (**19:4–5; Genesis 1:27–28; 2:24**)?

*Jesus directs the Pharisees to the Word.*

2. How does **verse 6** show that divorce is not part of God's plan? ✖

*two but one. They are no longer joined together... what God has joined together let no man separate*

3. Why then does **Deuteronomy 24:1–4** speak about divorce? When is a marriage bond broken? (See **19:9; 5:31–32.**)

*In the OT divorce was allowed b/c hearts were hardened — Marriage bond is broken when adultery occurs*

---

Jesus had narrowed the reasons for divorce to one, unchastity. The disciples, influenced by their society, thought there ought to be more reasons. If unchastity is the only reason for divorce, they thought, it would be better not to get married (**v. 10**).

According to God's Word, marriage is good and is God's plan for most people.

4. What advice does God's Word have when things strain the marriage bond? (See **Ephesians 5:21–33.**)

*submit to one another out of love for Jesus. Husbands love wives just as love own bodies*

5. What part does forgiveness play in strengthening the marriage bond?

*unconditional love submission*

6. Age is not a qualification for membership in the kingdom of heaven. The forgiveness that is given to members of the kingdom of heaven is needed by children also. (See **Psalm 14:3; Romans 3:12.**) What hint do **verses 13–15** give about how to qualify for forgiveness?

*innocence + faith depend on + trust Jesus*

# Applying the Message

1. Why is it hard for me to forgive others? What can I do to overcome this sin?

*stubbornness pride*

2. If I demand justice in all my relationships, what will I receive from God? from others?

3. It has been said that the hardest words to say are "I'm sorry" and the next hardest words are "I forgive you." When should I forgive those who have sinned against me? Immediately? After they show remorse? After they say that they are sorry?

4. How does partaking of the Lord's Supper strengthen me to receive and to give forgiveness?

5. I can show my appreciation for God's forgiveness in Christ in the following ways:

# Taking the Lesson Home

1. Look at **1 Corinthians 5:1–5** and **2 Corinthians 2:5–11**. See how an early Christian congregation used the steps of admonition.

2. Study the examples of forgiveness given by Jesus in **Luke 23:34** and by Stephen in **Acts 7:59–60.**

# Lesson 8

# Serve the King
# (Matthew 19:16–23:39)

## Approaching This Study

**Key verses:** "Whoever wants to become great among you must be your servant, and whoever wants to be first must be your slave—just as the Son of Man did not come to be served, but to serve, and to give His life as a ransom for many" **(Matthew 20:26–28).**

**Aim of this lesson:** To make service to Jesus and to our fellow humans, using our God-given talents, a goal for our lives.

## We Want to Be Great

*A missionary to a Native American tribe had his first opportunity to preach to the chief and several members of the tribe. As the missionary began explaining how God loved all people and sent His Son, Jesus, into the world on the first Christmas, the chief brought his tomahawk and laid it before the missionary and said, "I give my tomahawk to Jesus."*

*The missionary told how Jesus grew up and showed His love to people by healing their bodies and forgiving their sins. The chief came forward and laid his blanket before the missionary and said, "I give my blanket to Jesus."*

*As the missionary continued, he told about the crucifixion of Jesus. He told how wicked men nailed Jesus to the cross; how Jesus said, "Father, forgive them, for they do not know what they are doing"; how He gave His life and bowed His head in death. The chief disappeared for a minute and returned, leading his horse. He said, "I give my pony to Jesus."*

*Now the missionary told how Jesus was laid in the grave, but conquered death on Easter by rising from the dead, and that He has gone ahead to prepare a home in heaven for all who believe in Him. The chief walked forward, sat down before the missionary and said, "I give myself to Jesus."*

When we have been called into the kingdom of heaven and, by the working of the Holy Spirit, have received the free gift of forgiveness provided for us by Jesus Christ, we respond in loving service. "He died for all, that those who live should no longer live for themselves but for Him who died for them and was raised again" **(2 Corinthians 5:15)**.

What does it mean to live for Jesus? How can we serve Him?

Jesus, the promised King, said that anyone who wanted to be great in the kingdom of heaven should follow His example and be the servant of all.

Show us how to be great in Your kingdom, Jesus!

# Working with the Text

## The King Talks about Earning Eternal Life

Read **Matthew 19:16–30.**

1. To which Commandments did Jesus direct the young man who asked about eternal life?

2. What did Jesus say should be the motive for keeping His Commandments in **John 14:15?**

3. Why had the young man thought he had kept the Commandments?

4. Which Commandment had he not kept? (See **Matthew 22:37.**)

5. Who and what did this young man serve?

6. What are some of the dangers of riches according to **1 Timothy 6:9–10?**

7. What did Jesus promise to the believers who serve Him **(19: 28–30)?**

## The King Tells a Parable

Read **Matthew 20:1–16.**

The Parable of the Laborers in the Vineyard follows the question of Peter, "What then will there be for us?"

1. In this Kingdom parable, who is meant by the landowner? Who are the hired men?

2. What's unique about the goodness of God as He deals with people? What does God give to all who believe in His Son? (See **John 3:16.**)

3. Is Kingdom work a privilege or a duty? Why?

## The King Speaks of Greatness

Read **Matthew 20:17–28.**

1. What was the request of the mother of James and John? What may have been her understanding of the Kingdom? (See **Acts 1:6.**)

2. Why did the other disciples respond as they did in **verse 24?**

3. What is meant by the "cup" **(v. 22)?** (Also see **Matthew 26:39.**)

4. How did the Gentiles view greatness **(v. 25)?** What is the contrast between the world's idea of greatness and Jesus' teaching on greatness?

5. Study the following Scripture passages, and discuss the different examples of service Jesus has given us to follow: **Matthew 15:30, 32; John 11:17–27; 13:1–17; 19:25–27.**

6. How did Jesus give His life in service for many **(20:18–19)?** (Also see **John 19:30; 1 Timothy 2:3–6.**)

## The King, Son of David
Read **Matthew 20:29–34.**
This is the first time that Jesus publicly acknowledges and answers to the title "Son of David."
1. What is meant by this title? (See **Acts 2:29–32.**)

2. What does it mean to have mercy upon someone? What example of mercy does Jesus leave for us to follow?

## The King Enters
Read **Matthew 21:1–11.**
1. What examples of service to Jesus can be found in the Palm Sunday event?

2. What prophecy was fulfilled from **Isaiah 62:11** and **Zechariah 9:9?**

3. What did the crowds acknowledge about Jesus in their shouting **(Matthew 21:9)?**

Notice that the honor that came to Jesus on Palm Sunday came because of His humble, willing service.

## The King's Temple
Read **Matthew 21:12–22.**
1. What disservice to God had been taking place in the temple?

2. In what way were the children serving Jesus **(v. 15)?**

3. Why should children also be present in the congregation during worship **(v. 16)?**

4. Bethany was the home of Mary, Martha, and Lazarus. In what way had Mary and Martha served Jesus? (See **Luke 10:38–42.**)

## Questioning the King's Authority
Read **Matthew 21:23–27.**
1. As Jesus served people by teaching them, He was challenged by the religious leaders. What was the challenge **(v. 23)?**

2. What possible answers could they give to the counterquestion of Jesus in **verse 25?**

3. If they had believed that John was sent by God, what would they have done? (See **Matthew 3:2.**)

## More Parables from the King
Read **Matthew 21:28–22:14.**

1. This section contains three parables. To whom were they addressed **(21:45)?**

2. Who do you think is meant by the two sons **(vv. 28, 31–32)?**

3. What did Jesus expect of His listeners **(v. 32)?**

4. Who is meant by the landowner? Who are the tenants? Who is the son **(vv. 33–38, 43)?**

5. Jesus quoted **Psalm 118:22–23.** Who is the stone in **verse 42?** (See **Acts 4:10–12.**)

6. What will be the result of the Jews' rejection of Jesus **(v. 43)?**

7. How did the religious leaders show that they totally rejected Jesus (vv. 45–46)?

8. Explain the spiritual meaning of the Parable of the Wedding Banquet (22:2–14). The wedding clothes were provided as a free gift to all. The man without wedding clothes refused to accept this gift from the king. See **Romans 3:19–20, 28.** What wedding clothes do we all need?

# Enemies Attempt to Trap the King

Read **Matthew 22:15–45.**

The enemies of Jesus planned to trap Him. This section records three such attempts.

1. How did Jesus answer the question asked in **verse 17?** How do Christians serve government?

2. What teaching of the Kingdom did the Sadducees deny **(v. 23)?**

3. Posing a hypothetical situation regarding levirate marriage, the Sadducees sought to discredit Jesus. (For an explanation of the levirate marriage laws see **Deuteronomy 25:5–7**). The Sadducees accepted as God's Word only the first five books of the Scriptures, the writings of Moses. What did Jesus teach them from **Exodus 3:6?**

4. Jesus answered the question of the lawyer in **22:36** by quoting **Deuteronomy 6:5.** What should be the motivation to serve God and man?

5. How many of the Commandments are covered by Jesus' answer?

6. What can we learn about Jesus in **verses 42–44?**

7. Jesus' quotation in **22:44** is from **Psalm 110:1.** What important teaching about the Scriptures do we find in **22:43?**

## The King Proclaims Seven Woes

Read **Matthew 23:1–39.**

1. What controlled the actions of the teachers of the law and the Pharisees?

2. List several ways in which Jesus pointed to their religious showmanship.

3. What direction for greatness did Jesus give in **verses 11–12?**

4. For what sin did Jesus pronounce the woes upon the religious leaders?


5. The NIV lists seven woes pronounced upon the teachers of the law and the Pharisees. How, specifically, were these people doing a disservice to the kingdom of God?


6. What beautiful picture from nature is Jesus referring to in **verse 37?** What emotions does Jesus show in this verse? What is Jesus' will even for the people who reject Him?


# Applying the Message

1. In what ways can my attitude toward material possessions and my use of them show my faith?


2. What has my loyalty and service to Jesus cost me?


3. How have I been influenced by things that the world considers great? How does **John 15:5** guide me to understand true greatness before God?

4. What sins of hypocrisy could Jesus expose in my life? What can help me to recognize my true motivations?

5. In what ways can I love God with all my heart? soul? mind? How can I love my neighbor as myself?

6. One admonition often given to people is "Practice what you preach." How would this pertain to a believer?

7. What special gifts do I have that I can use to serve Jesus and my fellow human beings? How can I help others in my study group to recognize the gifts they each have?

# Taking the Lesson Home

1. Find examples of the world's great people in the areas of science, wealth, religion, society, politics, knowledge, crafts, and sports.
2. Study **Romans 13:1–10** to discover more about the relationship between church and state.
3. Look at the *Guinness Book of World Records* to see the futile ways in which people try to attain greatness.

# Lesson 9

# Inheriting the Kingdom
# (Matthew 24–25)

## Approaching This Study

**Key Verse:** "Then the King will say to those on His right, 'Come, you who are blessed by My Father; take your inheritance, the kingdom prepared for you since the creation of the world' " **(Matthew 25:34).**

**Aim of this lesson:** To observe with joy and faithful Christian living the signs of Jesus Christ's Second Coming, because by faith the kingdom of heaven belongs to us.

## We Need to Look Forward

*The owner of a large estate went to a foreign land to study and travel. He left his estate in the hands of a caretaker, who was faithful in its care and kept it in constant readiness for the owner's homecoming.*

*Although the owner was gone for many years, the caretaker patiently and faithfully did his work and enjoyed showing the estate to visitors.*

*One day after touring the grounds, a visitor asked the caretaker, "How long has the owner been away?"*

*"Seventeen years," the caretaker replied.*

*"You have kept everything so beautiful, as though you expected him to return home tomorrow," said the visitor.*

*The caretaker looked at the visitor and said, "Tomorrow, did you say? Not tomorrow! Today! He may return today!"*

Am I expecting Jesus to return today? Do I live as though I expect Jesus to come again soon? Do I look forward with joy to His Second Coming?

As Jesus revealed to His followers the signs preceding His Second Coming, He said, "At that time they will see the Son of Man coming in a cloud with power and great glory. When these things begin to take place, stand up and lift up your heads, because your redemption is drawing near" **(Luke 21:27–28).**

It is important that we, as citizens of the kingdom of heaven, read correctly the signs preceding Jesus Christ's Second Coming. We must heed His warnings, patiently wait, and faithfully work in joyous anticipation of His return to take us to the promised inheritance of eternal life in heaven.

# Working with the Text
## The King Tells about His Return
Read **Matthew 24:1–51.**

1. What was the topic of the conversation between Jesus and His disciples **(vv. 1–2)?**

2. What did Jesus predict would happen to the temple? What two things did the disciples ask Jesus about privately? Jesus answered both questions by telling of events to come. In these verses, which are the signs that shall occur in nature? Which are the signs that shall occur among the believers? List the warnings that Jesus gives to His followers.

3. What promises did He give to His followers **(vv. 13–14)?**

4. Jesus referred to **Daniel 9:27** and **11:31.** The temple in Jerusalem had already been defiled by a pagan idol and a pagan altar. Jesus pointed ahead to the destruction of Jerusalem by the Romans, which occurred in A.D. 70. How suddenly would the destruction come? How complete would the destruction of the temple be?

5. What picture is given in **Isaiah 13:10?** Why do you think many people will mourn when the Son of Man comes with power and great glory **(v. 30)?**

6. Who sends out the angels, and what will they do?

7. What lesson can we learn from the fig tree?

8. What will outlast this world?

9. What does **verse 36** tell Jesus' followers about the Last Day?

10. What attitude did the people of Noah's day have toward the warning about the flood?

11. If the thief had announced his coming, what would the homeowner have done?

12. What are the instructions for Jesus' followers in **verses 42–44?**

13. In what ways are the wise and the wicked servants different **(vv. 45–51)?**

# More Parables from the King

Read the Parable of the Ten Virgins in **Matthew 25:1–13.**
1. How is the Second Coming of Jesus pictured in this parable?

2. Jesus calls us to individual watchfulness in this parable. How does **Matthew 7:21–23** shed light on this parable?

3. What single word tells the main lesson of this parable?

Read the Parable of the Talents in **Matthew 25:14–30.**
4. As we search for spiritual meaning in this parable, who is the man (master)? Who are the servants? What does the master expect from his ser-

vants? What compliment do the first two servants receive? Why is the one-talent man condemned?

5. What is the main message of this parable?

# When the King Comes Again

Read **Matthew 25:31–46.**

1. What differences do you find between Jesus' Second Coming and His First Coming?

2. Who will be present on the Last Day?

3. Notice that the judgment has already taken place before a word is spoken. Who are the sheep? (See **John 10:27–28.**)

4. All people will be divided into two groups. How is the division made according to **John 3:36?**

5. What will be Jesus Christ's work on the Last Day?

6. What are the most joyous words that people will ever hear?

7. How does **verse 34** show that heaven is not earned by works?

8. How long had the Father been preparing this inheritance?

9. Why did Jesus refer to works? (See **Matthew 7:17–20; John 15:5; James 2:17.**)

10. How does faith show up in the believer's life? Who does Jesus say His followers serve when they serve others?

11. What are the most terrible words that a person can ever hear?

12. What is necessary before good works can count before God? (See **Hebrews 11:6.**)

13. How long will this separation from God last **(Daniel 12:2)?** For whom was hell created? (See **2 Peter 2:4.**) How do we know that God does not want people to be eternally lost? (See **Ezekiel 33:11; 2 Peter 3:9.**)

14. Use the following Scripture passages to describe eternal life in heaven: **Psalm 16:11; John 14:1–3; Revelation 7:9–17; 21:1–4.**

# Applying the Message

1. If someone asked me, "Are you going to heaven?" what would I answer? How can I be certain of my future with Jesus? (See **John 3:16.**)

2. Which of the signs that Jesus gave in these chapters do I see happening in the world today? in nature? in the church? in the lives of individuals and nations? What are these signs saying to me?

3. If someone scoffed at my faith in Jesus Christ's Second Coming, how would I answer? (Answer first and then look at **2 Peter 3:3–13.**)

4. What am I doing specifically to make it possible for people to inherit eternal life?

# Taking the Lesson Home

1. Read, pray, and sing hymns that speak about life everlasting.
2. For further study on the signs of Jesus Christ's Second Coming, see **Luke 21:5–36; 1 Timothy 4:1–4; 2 Timothy 3.**
3. Read **1 Corinthians 15:51–52** and **1 Thessalonians 4:16–17** for answers to questions about what will happen to the believers who are still living on the Last Day.

# Lesson 10

# The King Commands Us to Share the Kingdom (Matthew 26–28)

## Approaching This Study

**Key verses:** "Go and make disciples of all nations, baptizing them in the name of the Father and of the Son and of the Holy Spirit, and teaching them to obey everything that I have commanded you. And surely I am with you always, to the very end of the age" **(Matthew 28:19–20).**

**Aim of this lesson:** To grow in our understanding of Jesus' suffering, death, and resurrection so that we may appreciate what He has done for us and for every human being and, out of love and gratitude, share the Good News of the Kingdom in every possible way with other people.

## We Need to Tell

*"God created everything. After God had finished creating man and animals, He went up to the skies, never to return." That was all the Auca Indians of Ecuador knew about God.*

*Their lives were filled with fears and hate, murder and revenge. And, spearing by spearing, their tribe was becoming smaller and smaller in size.*

*Dayuma, the first Auca to become a believer, asked the question, "Why was I not caused to love the Lord Jesus long ago?"*

*She wanted to tell her mother about Jesus. "I will tell her lots, and then she will come to love Him lots."*

*But when the time came near to go back into the tribe with the Good News of Jesus, Dayuma was afraid. She was told, "You are the only one of your people who knows God. How will they hear if you don't go to tell them?"* (*Ethel Wallis,* The Dayuma Story)

God says in His Word, "How, then, can they call on the one they have not believed in? And how can they believe in the one of whom they have not heard?" **(Romans 10:14).**

Each of us knows people who do not believe in Jesus as their Savior and, like Dayuma in the preceding story, we may be fearful about our role in bringing the Good News to them. In our text for today, Jesus assures us we are not alone; neither are we without the authority and resources necessary to share the Gospel message.

# Working with the Text

## The Plot Against the King

Read **Matthew 26:1–13.**

Jesus, the promised King, knew what would happen to Him. The plan of God the Father to redeem and save His sinful and straying children had been revealed in the Scriptures. The words of **Isaiah 53** would be fulfilled. All this took place, not because people willed it, but because God willed it. "Yet it was the Lord's will to crush Him and cause Him to suffer, . . . the Lord makes His life a guilt offering" **(Isaiah 53:10).**

It was the time of the Passover, the Feast of Unleavened Bread. The Passover Feast commemorated the deliverance of the Israelites from the destroying angel when all the firstborn of the Egyptians were slain **(Exodus 12).** Those who were saved from death lived in houses that had the blood of a lamb painted over the door. Most likely John had the Passover lamb in mind when he said of Jesus, "Look, the Lamb of God, who takes away the sin of the world!" **(John 1:29).**

During those pre-Passover days, Jesus and His disciples stayed in Bethany and traveled back and forth to Jerusalem. A supper in Jesus' honor was given in Bethany. Lazarus, whom Jesus had raised from the dead, was there and Martha served **(John 12:2).**

1. What act of love did Mary do for Jesus **(26:7; John 12:3)**? For what other act is Mary of Bethany remembered? (See **Luke 10:39.**)

2. What act of kindness did Jesus say Mary was doing in **26:12?** What does this say to you about Mary's faith? How could Mary's act have been a comfort for Jesus at this time?

## The King Is Betrayed

Read **Matthew 26:14–25.**

1. The first time we hear Judas speak is in **John 12:5.** Satan was using money or riches to destroy Judas and (so he thought) Jesus, too. What did the Scriptures say about the betrayal of the Promised One? (See **Psalm 41:9; Zechariah 11:12–13**).

2. Thirty pieces of silver was the price of a slave **(Exodus 21:32)** and was the equivalent of four months' pay for the average worker. How did Jesus show concern for Judas' soul **(26:20–25)?**

## The King Shares a Meal with His Subjects

Read **Matthew 26:26–30.**

The covenant, or agreement, that God made with His people was signed with blood **(Exodus 24:4–8).** There was no blessed relationship with God without the shedding of blood **(Leviticus 17:11.)** How do the words of Jesus in **26:28** show that the shedding of blood in the Old Covenant pointed ahead to the shedding of His blood? (Also see **Hebrews 9:11–14.**)

After Jesus gave thanks for the wine and the flat, thin sheets of unleavened bread used in the Passover meal, He gave them to the disciples and said, "This is My body. This is My blood." Each time we celebrate the

Lord's Supper, we receive the body and blood of our Lord and Savior Jesus Christ together with the bread, and wine we remember His atoning sacrifice for us.

## The King Grieves

Read **Matthew 26:31–46.**

1. How do the words of Jesus on the way to Gethsemane show that He knew exactly what was going to happen?

2. What is the promise in **verse 32?**

3. Why was prayer especially important and necessary for Jesus on this Passover evening?

4. What verses show that Jesus was thoroughly and completely true man, yet without sin?

5. How do the words in **verse 40** show that Jesus was trying to help Peter overcome temptation and his overconfidence in himself?

## The King Is Arrested

Read **Matthew 26:47–56.**

1. There is scarcely a crime more distasteful to the human mind than betrayal. Nor is there a criminal more repulsive than a traitor. How did Jesus make a last effort to reach Judas' heart **(v. 50)?**

2. What verses show that Jesus was not taken against His will but that He volunteered? (Also see **John 18:4–9.**)

## The King Is Tried and Disowned

Read **Matthew 26:57–75.**

The night trial of Jesus had begun when He stood before the high priest and the Jewish court of elders and teachers of the law.

1. What verdict had already been decided upon **(v. 59)?**

2. **Deuteronomy 19:15** states that the evidence of two or three witnesses was needed to sustain a charge against a person. How was **Isaiah 53:7** fulfilled in the trial of Jesus?

3. But when Caiaphas, the high priest, put Jesus under oath to answer his question **(26:63),** Jesus plainly stated that He is true God. How did Jesus' answer in **verse 64** direct Caiaphas to the fulfillment of the prophecies in **Psalm 110:1** and **Daniel 7:13?**

4. How did the Jewish court continue to fulfill prophecy **(26:67–68; Isaiah 50:6)?**

5. How did Jesus show His love for Peter? (Also see **Luke 22:31–32, 61.**)

## The King's Betrayer Commits Suicide and the King Is Tried

Read **Matthew 27:1–26.**

The Jewish court was not allowed to carry out the death penalty. So Jesus was brought to Pilate, the Roman governor, for trial just as dawn was breaking.

1. What difference was there between Peter's sorrow over his sin and Judas' sorrow over his sin?

2. The accusation against Jesus changed from one court to the next. Of what did the Jewish elders accuse Jesus? (See **Luke 23:1–2.**)

3. How did Jesus' response to Pilate's question **(27:11)** differ from His response to the charges of the chief priests and elders?

4. Pilate found Jesus to be innocent **(Luke 23:4, 14),** yet he didn't have the courage to carry out his conviction. By what devious ways did he try to release Jesus? (See **27:15–26; Luke 23:6–7, 16.**)

## The King Is Killed

Read **Matthew 27:27–54.**

The Roman mode of executing anyone who wasn't a Roman citizen was crucifixion. Jesus had told His disciples and the other believers that He would be crucified.

1. How was the bronze serpent in **Numbers 21:8–9** a prophetic picture of Jesus? (See **John 3:14–15.**)

2. What other pictures of the crucifixion are found in **Psalm 22:16, 18; 69:21; Isaiah 53:12?**

3. Jesus hung on the cross from 9 a.m. to 3 p.m. What made Jesus' crucifixion different from the crucifixion of any other person? (Also see **Mark 15:22–38; Luke 23:34–46; John 19:26–33.**)

4. What was the testimony of the soldiers on duty at the crucifixion **(27:54)?**

## The King Is Buried

Read **Matthew 27:55–66.**
How was the prophecy of **Isaiah 53:9** fulfilled in the burial of Jesus?

## The King Rises from the Dead

Read **Matthew 28:1–15.**
Jesus had testified to His resurrection in many ways and at many times **(Matthew 12:40; 16:4, 21; 17:22–23; John 2:19.)** He died on Good Friday at 3 p.m. (first day). The Sabbath began at 6 p.m. of Friday and ended

at 6 p.m. on Saturday (second day). The first day of the week, Sunday, began at 6 p.m. on Saturday (third day).

1. How did the women react to the message of the angel?

2. How did the disciples react to the message of the women? (See **Luke 24:11.**)

3. How did the guards testify to the resurrection?

4. How many different people saw Jesus personally after His resurrection? (See **28:9; Luke 24:10, 13–15, 34, 36; John 20:26; 1 Corinthians 15:6–8.**)

## The King's Commission
Read **Matthew 28:16–20.**

The angel **(28:7),** and Jesus Himself **(28:10),** directed the disciples and the women and probably all the believers **(1 Corinthians 15:6)** to a special meeting with their risen Lord in Galilee.

1. What command did Jesus give to all believers **(vv. 18–20)?**

2. With whose power and authority are the believers to do this?

3. What does it mean to "make disciples of all nations"? In what two ways is this discipling done?

4. What does it mean to baptize in the name of the Father and of the Son and of the Holy Spirit? What does this teach us about the true God?

5. What promise of Jesus strengthens us to carry out the Great Commission?

# Applying the Message

Practice sharing your faith in Jesus as your Savior with another person in the study group.

1. The suffering and death of Jesus Christ are important to me because...

2. The resurrection of Jesus is important to me because …

3. How does the Holy Spirit help me as I share the Good News with others?

4. Since I am to make disciples of all nations, I will support and use the printed Word and religious radio and television programs in the following ways:

5. According to **Matthew 28:19–20,** all people are to be taught everything about God's kingdom. "Christian Education from the Cradle to the Grave" is the motto of some congregations. What needs do I have in the area of Christian education? How can I serve or help others in the area of Christian education?

6. I will personally share the Good News of the Kingdom in these ways with the following people:
my family

my neighbors

senior adults

youth

children

babies

7. The Lord has called me into His kingdom by faith in Jesus as my personal Savior. All of the blessings of the Kingdom are mine. How will I respond specifically to God's goodness in order to show my love and

thanks to Jesus, my King?

# Taking the Lesson Home

1. Study in detail the Feast of Unleavened Bread or Passover in **Exodus 12** as celebrated by the Jews. Note the fulfillment in Jesus, the promised King.

2. Using a concordance, study the passages in Scripture that speak of the necessity of the shedding of blood for the forgiveness of sins and salvation.

# MATTHEW

## His Kingdom Forever

**Leaders Notes**

# Leaders Notes

# Preparing to Teach Matthew

Read the text in a modern translation. The NIV is generally referred to in the lesson comments. You may also want to consult the introduction to the book of **Matthew** in the *Concordia Self-Study Bible*, and, if possible, read the *Concordia Self-Study Commentary (CPH, 1979)*.

In the section "Working with the Text" you as leader will guide discussion and the class's emphasis using the questions given (or others) to help the group discover what the text actually says. This is a major part of teaching, namely, directing the learners to discover for themselves. Another major portion of each lesson is helping the participant, by discussion, to see the meaning for our times, for our church and world today, and especially for our own lives.

## Group Bible Study

Group Bible study means mutual learning from one another under the guidance of a leader or facilitator. The Bible is an inexhaustible resource. No one person can discover all it has to offer. In a class many eyes see many things and can apply them to many life situations. The leader should resist the temptation to "give the answers" and so act as an "authority." This teaching approach stifles participation by individual members and can actually hamper learning. As a general rule the teacher is not to "give interpretation" but to "develop interpreters." Of course there are times when the leader should and must share insights and information gained by his or her own deeper research. The ideal class is one in which the leader guides class members through the lesson and engages them in meaningful sharing and discussion at all points, leading them to a summary of the lesson at the close. As a general rule, don't explain what the learners can discover by themselves.

Have a chalkboard and chalk or newsprint and marker available to emphasize significant points of the lesson. Put your inquiries or the inquiries of participants into questions, problems, or issues. This provokes thought. Keep discussion to the point. List on the chalkboard or newsprint the answers given. Then determine the most vital points made in the discussion. Ask additional questions to fill apparent gaps.

The aim of every Bible study is to help people grow spiritually, not merely in biblical and theological knowledge, but in Christian thinking and living. This means growth in Christian attitudes, insights, and skills for Christian living. The focus of this course must be the church and the world of our day. The guiding question will be, "What does the Lord teach us for life today through the book of **Matthew?**"

## Pace Your Teaching

Do not try to cover every question in each lesson. This will lead to undue haste and frustration. Be selective. Pace your teaching. Spend no more than five minutes in "Approaching This Study" and the introductory activity. Take time to go into the text topic by topic, but not word by word. Get the sweep of meaning. Occasionally stop to help the class gain understanding of a word or concept. Allow 15 minutes in "Applying the Message" and five minutes for "Taking the Lesson Home." This schedule, you will notice, allows only 35 minutes for "Working with the Text."

Should your group have more than a one-hour class period, you can take it more leisurely. But do not allow any lesson to "drag." Keep it moving. Keep it alive. Keep it meaningful. Eliminate some questions and restrict yourself to those questions most meaningful to the members of the class. If most members study the text at home, they can report their findings, and the time gained can be used to relate the lesson to life.

## Good Preparation

Good preparation by the leader usually affects the pleasure and satisfaction the class will experience.

## Suggestions to the Leader for Using the Study Guide
### The Lesson Pattern

This set of 10 lessons is based on a significant and timely New Testament book—the Gospel according to **Matthew.** The material is designed to aid *Bible study*, that is, to aid a consideration of the written Word of God, with discussion and personal application growing out of the text at hand. The typical lesson is divided into five sections:

1. Approaching This Study
2. An Introduction
3. Working with the Text
4. Applying the Message
5. Taking the Lesson Home

"Approaching This Study" and the introduction give the leader assistance in arousing the interest of the group in the concepts of the chapter. Current events and conditions are cited to "warm up" the class and convince its members that the Word of God spoken through **Matthew** is relevant to their present situation. Here the leader stimulates minds. Do not linger too long over the introductory remarks. Merely show that the chapters to be studied are meaningful to Christian faith and life today.

"Working with the Text" provides the real "spadework" necessary for Bible study. Here the class digs, uncovers, and discovers; it gets the facts and observes them. Comment from the leader is needed only to the extent that it helps the group understand the text. The same is true of looking up the indicated parallel passages. The questions in the Study Guide, arranged under subheadings and corresponding to sections within the text, are intended to help the learners discover the meaning of the text.

Having determined what the text says, the class is ready to apply the message. This is done, as the Study Guide suggests, by taking the truths found in **Matthew** and applying them to the world and Christianity in general and then to personal Christian life. Class time will not permit discussion of all questions and topics. In preparation the leader will select two or three and focus on them. These questions bring God's message to the individual Christian. Close the session by reviewing one important truth from the lesson.

Section 5, "Taking the Lesson Home," supplies the stimulated participant with guidelines for enrichment work at home. Suggestions are given for review, preview of the upcoming lesson, and for private study of topics related to the lesson. Give class members who complete some of these activities the opportunity to report briefly on their findings when the subject comes up in the next session.

Remember, the Word of God is sacred, but the Study Guide is not. The guide offers only suggestions. The leader should not hesitate to alter the guidelines or substitute others to meet his or her needs and the needs of the participants. Adapt your teaching plan to your class and to your class period. The first lesson suggests more presentation by the leader since it is introductory.

As you prepare, mark those sections which suggest a class activity. Choose the verses that should be looked up in Scripture. What discussion questions will you ask? at what points? Write them in the margin of your study book. Involve class members, but give them clear directions. What practical actions will you propose for the week following the lesson?

How will you best use your teaching period? Do you have 45 minutes? an hour? or 1 1/2 hours? If time is short, what should you cut? Learn to become a wise steward of class time.

# Lesson 1
## The King (Matthew 1–2)

## Approaching This Study

Read aloud or invite a volunteer to read aloud the "Key verses" and the "Aims of this lesson."

## We Need to Belong

Read aloud and briefly discuss the opening story. Ask, **What evidence do we find in today's society that people want to belong?** After a few moments of discussion, read aloud the final paragraphs of this section that introduce the Gospel according to **Matthew**.

## Working with the Text

This section of each lesson covers a large portion of Scripture. You may wish to use one of the following methods to cover the suggested readings.

1. Read the suggested portions of **Matthew** and discuss the questions that follow each reading with the entire class.

2. Assign the readings and the discussion questions to small groups. Allow time for the small groups to share their answers to the questions with the entire class.

3. Read the suggested portions of **Matthew** with the entire class. Then have small groups discuss the questions and share their answers with the entire class.

4. Assign a different reading and the corresponding questions to each small group. Allow time for the small groups to share their findings with the entire class.

5. Select only portions of the suggested readings.

### The Genealogy of the King

Read aloud **Matt. 1:1–17.** Then discuss the questions that follow.

1. Matthew begins his gospel with "A record of the genealogy of Jesus Christ." The central figure of Matthew's writing is announced in the first verse.

2. Matthew links the story of Jesus Christ with the history of God dealing with His people. Matthew traces the story of God's blessing, which begins with the free grace of His blessing to Abraham.

3. The genealogy is literally the "book of the generations" or "history of the origin." The genealogy links God's promises to their fulfillment in the person and work of Jesus Christ.

4. The verses provide evidence that God keeps His promises—the promise of a Savior first given to Adam and Eve in **Genesis 3** and the promise of salvation given to Abraham. Matthew proclaims the Christ as the climax of the history of God's mercy to His people. God has been in control of history.

## The Birth of the King

1. Mary was "with child through the Holy Spirit." Mary had no sexual encounter prior to or during her pregnancy.

2. The child conceived in Mary was from the *Holy Spirit*. All this took place to fulfill what the *Lord* (the Father) had said through the prophets. Jesus will be called "Immanuel"—which means "God with us."

3. Answers will vary. Emphasize the fact that Jesus was both true man and true God.

4. The angel told Joseph not to be afraid to take Mary home as his wife. Joseph's change of plans and obedience to God's command are evidence of his faith.

5. *Jesus* is the Greek form of the Hebrew name *Joshua* which means "Yahweh (the Lord God of the covenant) is salvation."

6. Jesus was the once and for all sacrifice for sin. Jesus was slaughtered for our sin. Jesus' punishment brought us peace. By Jesus' wounds we are healed.

7. Jesus is "God with us" in the fullest sense. Jesus was true God.

8. The virgin birth of Jesus as foretold by the prophets is the culmination of God's plan for salvation. The virgin birth accentuates the fact that Jesus was true God. Jesus came to earth to do that which is impossible for us—to live a perfect life under God's Law. Jesus then took the full wrath of God's anger toward our sin as He suffered and died on the cross. Jesus received that which we deserved—death—and we receive that which Jesus deserved—eternal life.

## Wise Men Visit the King

1. Jerusalem was the hub of Judaism. The wise men followed a star searching for the King of the Jews. It was only natural for them to seek the King of the Jews in Jerusalem, the headquarters for Judaism.

2. Herod the Great was a non-Jew, who was appointed king of Judea by the Roman Senate in 40 B.C. and had gained control in 37. Like most rulers of the day, he was ruthless, murdering his wife, his three sons, mother-in-law, brother-in-law, uncle, and many others—not to mention the babies in Bethlehem **(Matt. 2:16).** Herod feared anyone who might threaten his rule.

3. The Jewish religious leaders knew that the Messiah would be born in

Bethlehem because Micah had prophesied this seven centuries earlier (**Micah 5:2**).

4. **Num. 24:17** indicated that Israel's Deliverer would be like a star. The wise men were miraculously led by His star.

5. Details of the wise men's worship are not provided. We do know that in response to God's love revealed to the wise men in the Christ Child, the wise men presented the child with gifts—gold, incense, and myrrh.

6. Answers will vary. The faith of the wise men caused them to follow the star for a great distance, return to their country by another route, and share gifts with the child.

### The King Escapes and Returns

1. An angel appeared to Joseph in a dream to tell him to flee to Egypt. After Herod died, an angel again appeared to Joseph to tell him to return to Israel. When Archelaus began his reign, the angel told Joseph to leave Judea. Joseph took his family to live in a town called Nazareth.

2. The rulers of Israel opposed the kingdom of Jesus Christ because they believed it threatened their earthly kingdom. Today people continue to oppose Jesus' kingdom as they reject the Holy Spirit who works through God's Word to create saving faith, turn away from God and His will, make decisions that are in opposition to God's Word, deny God, or create and worship gods (self, money, property, etc.) other than the one true God.

## Applying the Message

1. Answers will vary. Emphasize the fact that God chose them by the power of the Holy Spirit.

2. Answers will vary. Affirm the fact that God keeps His promises.

3. Through faith, God makes us wise—unto salvation, to choose that which God desires, to serve Him through our words and actions.

4. Answers will vary. Both Mary and Joseph listened to God and did as He said. In the most trying circumstances, Mary and Joseph continued to believe God's promises.

5. Answers will vary. Urge participants to list specific things they can do to share Jesus Christ with others.

## Taking the Lesson Home

Urge interested participants to complete one or more of the suggested activities to reinforce and enrich the concepts taught in this lesson.

# Lesson 2
## The Change (Matthew 3–4)

## Approaching This Study
Read aloud or invite a volunteer to read aloud the "Key verse" and the "Aims of this lesson."

## We Need to Change
Read aloud and briefly discuss the opening story and related questions.

1. Neither the bandit nor community experienced a change of faith. Their behavior was merely a response to their outward circumstances.

2. Ask, **How is it possible for us, who are unable to obey God perfectly, to be qualified to receive blessings that are intended only for those who are holy?** Affirm the responses that point to the work of Christ Jesus and those that underscore the complete change God brings to all who repent and come to faith through the working of the Holy Spirit.

## Working with the Text
### Preparing the Way
Invite a participant to read **Matt. 3:1–12** aloud to the group. Continue with a discussion of the questions that follow.

1. John the Baptizer was the son of Zechariah and Elizabeth, born to them when they were both well along in years **(Luke 1:13).** Zechariah prophesied about John, calling him a prophet of the Most High who would prepare the way for the Savior **(Luke 1:76–79).** After John grew up, he lived in the desert until he began his public ministry **(Luke 1:80).**

2. John preached in the desert; he preached repentance; his clothes were made of camel's hair with the leather belt around his waist; his food was locusts and wild honey. Invite a volunteer to read **Is. 40:1–3.** Comment on the privilege John had as the prophesied forerunner who would prepare the people for the coming Savior, who in turn would bring the comfort of forgiveness, life, and salvation.

3. John's role was to prepare the hearts of the people to receive the Messiah.

4. The one word summary of the preaching of John is *repent.*

5. In order for human hearts to be ready to receive the forgiveness, hope, and comfort of the Gospel, they must first, by the power of the Holy Spirit, recognize, acknowledge, and repent of their sinfulness. This change precedes the change the Spirit works when He imparts to us forgiveness,

life, and salvation through the merits of Christ Jesus our Lord.

6. Christ Jesus came to give Himself as the once and for all sacrifice to take away the sins of the world **(John 1:29)**.

7. Peter replied, "Repent and be baptized, every one of you, in the name of Jesus Christ for the forgiveness of your sins. And you will receive the gift of the Holy Spirit" **(Acts 2:38)**.

8. Forgiven by God and empowered by the Holy Spirit, God's people produce fruit in keeping with repentance **(3:8)**.

9. As evidence of an alive faith, John offered the following examples: The man with two tunics should share with him who has none, and the one who has food should do the same; tax collectors should not collect any more than they are required to; soldiers shouldn't extort money or accuse people falsely and should be content with their pay.

10. John indicates that sincere believers are those who produce fruit in keeping with repentance while hypocrites have a religion in form and tradition (i.e., "We have Abraham as our father") but lack a personal faith.

11. The baptism of John was a baptism of repentance.

12. John's testimony about the promised King and His work included the following: The promised King would be greater than he (John said he was not even worthy to carry the King's sandals—**v. 11b**); He would baptize with the Holy Spirit and with fire (a prophecy of Pentecost) **(v. 11c)**; and He will come to judge the world, separating the faithful from the unbelievers **(v. 12)**.

## The Baptized King

Invite a volunteer to read **Matthew 3:13–17** aloud to the group. Continue with a discussion of the questions in this section and in the three sections immediately following. If you choose to do so, assign each of these sections to a small group. Then after five minutes or so, reassemble participants in a large group and briefly review the Bible readings and questions in each section.

1. Jesus asked John to baptize him **(v. 13)**.

2. John tried to deter Jesus, stating that he should be baptized by Jesus, rather than Jesus being baptized by him **(v. 14)**.

3. Jesus insisted on being baptized in order to fulfill all righteousness **(v. 15)**. This was part of His keeping the Law perfectly in our place.

## The King Is Tempted

1. Jesus was led into the desert to be tempted by the devil **(v. 1)**. Jesus was tempted as we are but He resisted temptation, fulfilling righteousness in our place by remaining obedient to God at all times.

2. First, the devil tempted Jesus to satisfy Himself with physical com-

forts, questioning whether Jesus was truly the Son of God. Next, the devil tempted Him to put God's care to the test. Then Jesus was promised all the kingdoms of the world if He would but worship the devil.

3. With every assault, Jesus countered with an appropriate quotation from God's Word. Mention that God also empowers us to resist the devil and his temptations through His Word.

### The King Begins His Ministry

1. When Jesus heard that John had been put in prison, He returned to Galilee **(v. 12)**.

2. Jesus told the people, "Repent for the kingdom of heaven is near" **(v. 17)**.

### The King Calls and Heals

1. When Jesus said, "I will make you fishers of Men," He meant that He would equip the disciples to be His pastors and evangelists whose goal it would be to catch people with the Good News of salvation.

2. Jesus went throughout Galilee, teaching in their synagogues, preaching the Good News of the kingdom, and healing every disease and sickness among the people **(v. 23)**.

## Applying the Message

Proceed with the questions in this section as a large group. Comment that the discussion questions here are designed to help us apply the portion of **Matthew** studied today to our daily lives.

1–2. These questions are designed for individual and private reflection. Invite participants to share any comments or further questions these items evoke.

3. Reviewing and reflecting upon the Ten Commandments, we are reminded over and over again of our failure to keep them.

4. We confess Jesus Christ as Lord solely by the power of the Holy Spirit.

5–8. Invite participants to share responses, insights, or comments if they choose to do so.

## Closing Prayer Suggestion

Pray together the prayer suggestion in the Study Guide.

## Taking the Lesson Home

Urge interested participants to complete one or more of the suggested activities to reinforce and enrich the concepts taught in this lesson.

# Lesson 3

## Blessedness (Matthew 5–7)

## Approaching This Study

Read aloud or invite a volunteer to read aloud the "Key verse" and the "Aim of this lesson."

## We Want to Be Happy and Prosperous

Read aloud and briefly discuss the opening story. Invite participants to share their own definition or example of *blessing* with the group. Affirm real blessings as those things received in gratitude to God for all He has given us through Christ Jesus our Lord.

## Working with the Text

### Blessed Are . . .

Invite a volunteer to read **Matt. 5:1–11** aloud to the group. You may choose to do the eight topics in this section as a whole class, or divide the class into small groups, inviting each group to study one or more of the topics and report back to the whole group. Possible answers to the discussion questions in each section follow.

### . . . The Poor in Spirit (v. 3)

1. Jesus said, "Blessed are the *poor* in spirit, for theirs is the kingdom of heaven."

2. The poor in spirit are those who possess broken and contrite hearts. They are bankrupt in the value they place on themselves or the things of this world and find Jesus and His gift of forgiveness, life, and salvation as their treasure.

3. Spiritually proud individuals may be proud of their piety or achievements in their religious life. A spiritually poor person is someone who recognizes his or her unworthiness before the Lord. By God's grace and through the working of the Holy Spirit, the end result is that the spiritually poor person receives the riches of God's grace which are offered freely to all through the merits of Christ.

4. The kingdom of heaven is a spiritual kingdom, a communion of believers in union with Jesus Christ. Jesus Christ is the Head, the King, and the blessings of this kingdom are the sum total of all the gifts of God in Christ Jesus as they are enjoyed here on earth in the Christian church and, finally, above in the kingdom of glory.

5. People remain poor in spirit as long as they recognize their sinfulness, confess their sins, and in faith receive the benefits of Christ's redemptive work on our behalf.

## . . . Those Who Mourn (v. 4)

1. **Verse 4** says, "Blessed are those who mourn."

2. Accept participants' responses. Christians mourn over all the manifestations of sin in their lives and in the world around them.

3. Jesus was to comfort all who mourn **(Is. 61:2)**.

4. Our God is the Father of compassion and the God of all comfort. He comforts us in all our troubles, so that we can comfort those in any trouble with the comfort we ourselves have received from God. Just as the sufferings of Christ flow over into our lives, so also through Christ our comfort overflows **(2 Cor. 1:3–5)**.

## . . . The Meek (v. 5)

1. Accept participants' thoughts on the meaning of the word *meek*. Comment that meekness here refers to an attitude of humility toward God as well as in our relationships with others.

2. Answers may vary. Generally, the world affirms a take charge, go-for-it approach which stands in contrast to meekness.

3. The attitude of Jesus is described in **1 Peter 2:22–24** as follows: "He committed no sin, and no deceit was found in His mouth." When they hurled their insults at Him, He did not retaliate; when He suffered, He made no threats. Instead, He entrusted Himself to Him who judges justly."

4. **Ps. 37:10–11** contrasts meekness with wickedness.

5. Answers may vary. Affirm God's promise of blessings for this world as well as the next for those who, as the Spirit works in them through the means of grace, demonstrate a spirit of meekness in the lives they live for Him.

6. In order to avoid conflict between the two households, Abraham placed the desires of his nephew, Lot, ahead of his own. Participants may reflect on their own willingness to demonstrate meekness in a similar situation.

7. Christ's examples of meekness include the following: "You have heard that it was said, 'Eye for eye, and tooth for tooth.' But I tell you, Do not resist an evil person. If someone strikes you on the right cheek, turn to him the other also. And if someone wants to sue you and take your tunic, let him have your cloak as well. If someone forces you to go one mile, go with him two miles. Give to one who asks you, and do not turn away from the one who wants to borrow from you" **(Matt. 5:38–42)**.

8. Although the love of Christ compels us to regard the needs of others

ahead of our own, God also empowers us to be bold in defending the cause of righteousness as Christ Himself exemplified when He drove out those who were changing money and selling in the temple courts.

9. Accept participants' responses. Comment that demonstrating "power under control" requires self-discipline and faithfulness—characteristics that evidence the working of the Holy Spirit in the life of a Christian **(Gal. 5:22–23)**.

## . . . Those Who Hunger and Thirst for Righteousness **(v. 6)**

1. Abraham's righteousness was the righteousness of Christ, the promised Savior—righteousness God gave Abraham by grace through faith. "[Abraham] believed God and it was credited to him as righteousness" **(Gal. 3:6)**.

2. Christ Jesus earned our righteousness for us. His innocent life, death, and resurrection paid for the sins of the world.

3. As God's Holy Spirit works in our hearts, we grow in the desire to know, love, and serve Him better.

4. Jesus speaks of the righteousness that comes through faith in Him. Persons with the gift of saving faith honor God by obeying the spirit of the Law and the letter of the Law as we are empowered by the Spirit of God.

5. Jesus calls us to live God-pleasing lives as evidence of Him as the mainstay and chief support in the life of all who believe. Examples of the fruit of faith produced in the life of a Christian will vary.

## . . . The Merciful **(v. 7)**

1. The Lord is compassionate and gracious, slow to anger, abounding in love and faithfulness, maintaining love to thousands, and forgiving wickedness, rebellion, and sin.

2. Zechariah, in poetic language, praised God who in His mercy sent the Savior to rescue His people so that we might serve Him without fear in holiness and righteousness all our days.

3. Jesus "had to be made like His brothers in every way, in order that He might become a merciful and faithful high priest in service to God, and that He might make atonement for the sins of the people" **(Heb. 2:17)**.

4. God's mercy shows itself in the lives of God's people, enabling them to show love for one another and for those outside the fellowship of believers—including enemies. As we ask God, confident in His love for us in Christ, He will give us mercy and grace to help us in our time of need **(Heb. 4:16)**.

## . . . The Pure in Heart **(v. 8)**

1. Jesus described the natural heart as emitting evil thoughts, murder,

adultery, sexual immorality, theft, false testimony, and slander **(Matt. 15:19)**.

2. Jeremiah described the human heart as "deceitful above all things and beyond cure" **(Jer. 17:9)**.

3. God desires that sinners repent, rid themselves of all the offenses they have committed, and get a new heart and a new spirit, so they may live **(Ezek. 18:30–32)**.

4. God says, "I will give them an undivided heart and put a new spirit in them; I will remove from them their heart of stone and give them a heart of flesh" **(Ezek. 11:19)**. Changing hearts is the work of the Holy Spirit through the Gospel.

5. God's Spirit moves believers to love God and others.

6. In heaven the hearts of God's people are perfectly pure and obedient.

### . . . The Peacemakers **(v. 9)**

1. Jesus is described as the Prince of Peace. His kingdom is eternal.

2. Peace was part of the message of the angels as they announced the Savior's birth to the shepherds in the fields of Bethlehem.

3. Paul described the peace of Jesus, telling of the reconciliation He brought in the relationship between God and fallen humanity. In his letter to the Philippians, Paul called this peace that which transcends all understanding, praying that this peace would guard the hearts and minds of believers in Christ Jesus. We can be ambassadors of this peace by living and sharing the Good News of Jesus.

4. God's Spirit enables us to demonstrate kindness and compassion to one another, forgiving each other, just as in Christ God has forgiven us.

### . . . Those Who Are Persecuted **(v. 10)**

1. Isaiah prophesied that the Messiah would be despised and rejected by men, a man of sorrows, and familiar with suffering. He took up our infirmities and carried our sorrows, yet we considered Him stricken by God, smitten by Him, and afflicted. He was pierced for our transgressions, He was crushed for our iniquities; the punishment that brought us peace was upon Him, and by His wounds we are healed. Jesus lived, suffered, and died for us.

2. Just as Christ suffered for doing good, even so we also have been called to suffer, following His example.

3. After the apostles were flogged, they rejoiced because they had been counted worthy of suffering disgrace for the Name.

4. Allow participants to share the different ways persecution can come to people of God.

5. We should not be concerned over receiving a few scars because there

is a crown of righteousness in heaven (**2 Tim. 4:8**) awaiting the faithful.

Have volunteers take turns reading the remainder of the Sermon on the Mount to the class or invite participants to read it on their own. Continue with the next section.

## Applying the Message

Lead the whole group in a discussion of the questions in this section.

1. Being "poor in spirit" means finding one's sense of self in Him who died for us and rose again; it is not at all like struggling with feelings of inferiority. Having the Creator and ruler of the entire universe as our personal Savior and friend is the ultimate source for a healthy self-concept. At the Lord's Table Jesus gives faith-strengthening assurance to repentant hearts.

2. We can assure "those who mourn" of Christ's forgiveness, of His restoring power, and of His comfort for those who grieve. Point out the blessed hope of the resurrection for all who trust in Jesus as their Savior.

3. Encourage participants to make distinctions. The approach God would have His people take is one typified by unselfishness, kindness, and the ability to hope for the best and to bring out the best in others.

4. Accept participants' responses. Mention that honoring and valuing God's gifts to us is one way of thanking and praising Him for His goodness.

5–6. Invite participants to share if they desire to do so. Affirm the change the Holy Spirit brings as He works in us through the Word and sacraments—the means of grace.

## Taking the Lesson Home

Urge interested participants to complete one or more of the suggested activities to reinforce and enrich the concepts taught in this lesson.

# Lesson 4

## Follow the King (Matthew 8–10)

## Approaching This Study

Read aloud or invite a volunteer to read aloud the "Key verse" and the "Aim of this lesson."

# We Need a Purpose for Living

Read aloud and briefly discuss this opening segment. Ask, **What does it mean to follow Jesus?**

# Working with the Text

This section of each lesson covers a large portion of Scripture. You may wish to use one of the following methods to cover the suggested readings.

1. Read the suggested portions of **Matthew** and discuss the questions that follow each reading with the entire class.

2. Assign the readings and the discussion questions to small groups. Allow time for the small groups to share their answers to the questions with the entire class.

3. Read the suggested portions of **Matthew** with the entire class. Then have small groups discuss the questions and share their answers with the entire class.

4. Assign a different reading and the corresponding questions to each small group. Allow time for the small groups to share their findings with the entire class.

5. Select only portions of the suggested readings.

Invite a participant to read **Matt. 8:1–17** aloud to the group. Then read or paraphrase the paragraphs in this section of the lesson to the group. Ask participants to give examples from this portion of **Matthew** of the various ways Jesus showed Himself to be the Messiah, the Son of God.

## The Cost of Following the King

Invite a participant to read **Matt. 8:18–22** aloud to the group. Then read or paraphrase the paragraphs preceding the questions. Affirm the commitment Jesus gives to those who are called by faith to follow Him. Continue with a discussion of the questions.

1. Jesus did not want anyone to follow Him expecting the way to be easy. The faithfulness Jesus brings into the lives of His followers endures the lack of comfort and security, endures the hardship and persecution.

2. Followers of Jesus are not to be arrogant if they have earthly riches. Nor are they to put their hope in wealth, which is so uncertain. They are to put their hope in God, who richly provides us with everything for our enjoyment. They are to be rich in good deeds, generous, and willing to share. "In this way they will lay up treasure for themselves as a firm foundation for the coming age, so that they may take hold of the life that is truly life" **(1 Tim. 6:19).**

3. Jesus tells us not to worry about our physical needs being met; He

will take care of us. Jesus promises that the meek will inherit the earth **(Matt. 5:5)**.

4. The best way we can show our love for others is to bring the Gospel to them so they too may be saved.

5. Jesus desires to occupy the center and focus of the life, goals, ambitions, and aspirations of those who belong to Him.

## Miracles of the King

As a volunteer reads aloud **Matt. 8:23–9:8,** invite the class to listen for evidence that Jesus is true God.

Jesus showed Himself to be true God by calming the storm, healing two demon-possessed men, forgiving sin, and healing a paralyzed man.

## The King Calls Levi

Invite a participant to read the calling of Matthew **(Matt. 9:9–12)** aloud to the group.

1–2. Matthew, also known as Levi, was the son of Alphaeus and was a tax collector. He was collecting taxes when Jesus called him.

3. Matthew records that he "got up and followed Him" **(v. 9)**.

4. Accept participants' speculations.

5. Luke describes the celebration as a great banquet for Jesus at Matthew's house. In attendance were a large crowd of tax collectors and others. Mostly likely Matthew invited these business friends and associates so that they, too, could meet Jesus and come to faith in Him.

6. The Pharisees asked Jesus' disciples, "Why does your teacher eat with tax collectors and 'sinners'?" **(v. 11)**. Jesus responded, "It is not the healthy who need a doctor, but the sick. But go and learn what this means: 'I desire mercy, not sacrifice.' For I have not come to call the righteous, but sinners" **(vv. 12–13)**.

The sick are those who are convicted of their sinfulness and recognize their need for the Savior. The righteous are those who trust in their own righteousness and goodness and deny their need for Jesus.

7. Jesus words indicate His desire for the Pharisees to come to a right understanding of their condition so that they, too, would repent and be saved.

8. Being merciful toward others is a manifestation of the Holy Spirit at work in the lives of those who have already received the mercy of God by faith in Christ Jesus. The Pharisees were not merciful in their attitude toward those they thought to be the undesirables of society; neither had they permitted themselves to receive the benefits of God's mercy.

## The King Teaches about Fasting

Read or have a volunteer read **Matt. 9:14–17** aloud to the group. Continue by reading or paraphrasing the paragraph preceding the questions. Then discuss the questions.

1. Jesus said, "No one sews a patch of unshrunk cloth on an old garment, for the patch will pull away from the garment, making the tear worse. Neither do men pour new wine into old wineskins. If they do, the skins will burst, the wine will run out and the wineskins will be ruined. No, they pour new wine into new wineskins, and both are preserved" **(vv. 16–17)**.

2. A person who comes to faith is born again **(John 3:3)**, made a new creation in Christ **(2 Cor. 5:17)**, and given new birth into a living hope through the resurrection of Jesus Christ from the dead **(1 Peter 1:3)**.

## More Miracles by the King

Invite one or more participants to read **Matt. 9:18–38** aloud to the group. Then continue by discussing the questions provided in this section.

1. When He saw the crowds, He had compassion on them, because they were harassed and helpless, like sheep without a shepherd **(v. 36)**.

2. Jesus told His followers to "ask the Lord of the harvest, therefore, to send out workers into His harvest field" **(v. 38)**.

## The King Sends Out His Followers

Ask a volunteer to read **Matt. 10:1–15** aloud to the group. Proceed with a discussion of the questions in this section.

1. These are the names of the twelve apostles: first, Simon (who is called Peter) and his brother Andrew; James son of Zebedee, and his brother John; Philip and Bartholomew; Thomas and Matthew the tax collector; James son of Alphaeus, and Thaddaeus; Simon the Zealot and Judas Iscariot, who betrayed Him **(vv. 2–4)**. Mark adds that Jesus gave the brothers James and John the name *Boanerges*, which means "Sons of Thunder." Luke mentions Judas the son of James, who is referred to also as Thaddaeus.

2. Jesus called His twelve disciples to Him and gave them authority to drive out evil spirits and to heal every disease and sickness **(v. 1)**.

## The King Assigns a Task

Invite one or more participants to read **Matt. 10:16–33** aloud to the class. Read or paraphrase the introductory words in this section of the Student Pages before continuing with the questions.

1. Enemies of God's kingdom will persecute and punish the faithful, arrest them, and bring them before the authorities.

2. To meet the tactics of the enemy, believers are to "be as shrewd as snakes and as innocent as doves" **(v. 16)**. They are not to worry when under arrest as to what they will say or how they will say it because at that time the Spirit will give them the words to say **(vv. 19–20)**. Furthermore, believers are to stand firm to the end so they will be saved **(v. 22)**, and when persecuted in one place, they are to move on to another **(v. 23)**.

3. Jesus explains it this way, "A student is not above his teacher, nor a servant above his master. It is enough for the student to be like his teacher, and the servant like his master. If the head of the house has been called Beelzebub, how much more the members of his household!" **(vv. 24–25)**.

4. We are to handle our fear with confidence, trusting in God's love and care for us.

### The King . . . First in Our Lives

Ask a volunteer to read **Matt. 10:34–42** aloud to the rest of the group. Continue by reading or paraphrasing the introductory paragraph in the Students Pages. Then discuss the questions.

1. To be worthy of Jesus is to love Him more than father or mother, son or daughter—more than our very life.

2. To give our lives totally into the hands of Him who died for us and rose again is to find the ultimate purpose, peace, and reward.

3. The kinds of rewards Jesus speaks of include receiving the one who sent Jesus, a prophet's reward, and a righteous man's reward.

4. Great will be a crossbearer's reward in heaven.

## Applying the Message

Involve all participants in a discussion of these questions to help them apply the portion of God's Word studied in today's lesson.

1. Encourage participants to share their insights and examples from their own experiences. To break the ice, share some of your own.

2. Affirm that many of us place too high a priority on maintaining a comfortable existence. Accept participants' comments.

3. Those who enjoy the benefits of God's merciful forgiveness through Christ Jesus have the privileged task of sharing the Good News of God's forgiving grace with others. Invite volunteers to share a plan of action.

4. Invite comments. Point out that sometimes demonstrating concern involves the risk of taking a stand and initiating a confrontation.

5. Encourage sharing. Comment on the comfort Christ's presence brings in the midst of adversity, trials, and challenges.

6. The miracles remind us that as God's Son, Jesus has all power and authority in the world under His control and at His command. We will

always remain in His love and care even when called upon to pay the price of following Him.

## Taking the Lesson Home

Urge interested participants to complete one or more of the suggested activities to reinforce and enrich the concepts taught in this lesson.

# Lesson 5

## Listen to the King (Matthew 11–13)

## Approaching This Study

Read aloud or invite a volunteer to read aloud the "Key verse" and the "Aim of this lesson."

## We Need to Listen

Read aloud and briefly discuss the opening story. Invite volunteers to share examples from their own experiences of hearing but not listening. After a few moments of discussion, read aloud the final paragraphs of this introductory section.

## Working with the Text

This section of each lesson covers a large portion of Scripture. You may wish to use one of the methods suggested in previous sessions to cover the readings.

### The King's Servant

Invite a participant to read **Matt. 11:1–15.** Continue with a discussion of the questions that follow.

1. John's disciples asked Jesus, "Are you the one who was to come, or should we expect someone else?" **(v. 3).**

2. Jesus replied, "Go back and report to John what you hear and see: The blind receive sight, the lame walk, those who have leprosy are cured, the deaf hear, the dead are raised, and the good news is preached to the poor" **(vv. 4–5).** The **Isaiah** passages referenced in parentheses include the prophecies about the Messiah. In **Luke 4:16–21** Jesus clearly identifies Himself as the fulfiller of these prophecies.

3. By faith, through the working of the Holy Spirit they would recognize

Jesus as the promised Messiah.

## To Listen and to Understand

Ask one or more volunteers to read **Matt. 11:16–30** aloud to the group. Then read the brief paragraph and continue with a discussion of this section's questions.

1. Those who come to a saving faith in Jesus have also been given the characteristics of meekness and humility. Only those whom God has freed from self-reliance and conceit are able to trust in Jesus as their only Lord and Savior. In **verse 25** Jesus comments that God has hidden things from the wise and learned and revealed them to little children.

2. Spiritual knowledge and understanding is given by God and received through faith in Christ Jesus. We become acquainted with God the Father by becoming better acquainted with Jesus Christ, His Son.

3. Jesus wants to comfort and strengthen all who are in need. "Come to Me, all you who are weary and burdened, and I will give you rest. Take My yoke upon you and learn from Me, for I am gentle and humble in heart, and you will find rest for your souls. For My yoke is easy and My burden is light" **(Matt. 11:28–30)**.

4. Jesus wants to give His followers rest.

5. Jesus wants His followers to take His easy and light yoke and, in learning from Him, to find rest for their souls. Jesus promises to comfort, sustain, and support those who are His as they dedicate their lives to Him.

## The King of the Sabbath

Ask someone to read **Matt. 12:1–21** aloud to the group or invite everyone to read it silently to themselves. Continue with the questions.

1. "The Pharisees went out and plotted how they might kill Jesus" **(v. 14)**.

2. The prophecy from **Isaiah** describes the promised King as follows: "Here is My servant, whom I uphold, my chosen one in whom I delight" **(v. 1a)**. Isaiah also describes the work Jesus did in the Kingdom: "He will bring justice to the nations. He will not shout or cry out, or raise his voice in the streets. A bruised reed He will not break, and a smoldering wick He will not snuff out. In faithfulness He will bring forth justice...In His law the islands will put their hope" **(v. 1b–4)**.

## The King and His Foe

Have one or more volunteers read **Matt. 12:22–50.** Then discuss the questions included in this section.

1. The saving knowledge that Jesus is the Christ, the Son of the living God, is revealed by God the Father **(Matt. 16:17b)**. No one can confess

Jesus as Lord except by the power of the Holy Spirit **(1 Cor. 12:3)**.

2. Jesus said, "For as Jonah was three days and three nights in the belly of a huge fish, so the Son of Man will be three days and three nights in the heart of the earth" **(Matt. 12:40)**.

3. Those who listen and believe that Jesus is their promised King and Savior become members of the family of Jesus with all the rights and privilege of this close relationship with Him.

## The King Uses Parables To Teach

Continue with a reading of **Matt. 13:1–17.** Review the definition of a parable and the list of helpful points for the correct understanding of parables as printed in the Study Pages. Then proceed with a study of the parables included in this portion of Matthew's gospel.

## Parable of the Sower (vv. 3–23)

Review the questions accompanying this parable.

1. Jesus spoke in parables so that His words might be understood only by those possessing a saving faith in Him.

2. Accept participants' descriptions of the earthly meaning of the Parable of the Sower. Comment that in ancient times farmers broadcast their seed by simply throwing it out on the ground. The four different types of soil where the seed landed were the path, the rocky places, the thorny ground, and the good soil.

3. The seed is the Word of God.

4. Ultimately the sower of the seed is God Himself.

5. God continues sowing the Word as it is spoken, written, preached, and otherwise brought to those without faith.

6. The Word of God stands forever **(1 Peter 1:25)**. It is useful for teaching, rebuking, correcting, and training in righteousness **(2 Tim. 3:16)**. The Gospel is the power of God for the salvation of everyone who believes **(Rom. 1:16)**. It is a light for our feet and a light to our path **(Ps. 119:105)**.

7. Jesus says the following about discipleship: "If you hold to My teaching, You are really My disciples. Then you will know the truth, and the truth will set you free" **(John 8:31–32)**.

8. The first kind of hearer hears the Word but does not come to a saving faith because the devil comes and snatches it away before that happens.

9. The second kind of hearer is like seed that falls on rocky ground. This hearer hears the Word and at once receives it with joy. But since this hearer has no root, his or her faith lasts only a short time. **John 6:60–66** tells of some believers who stopped following Jesus because they did not possess faith—the life-giving gift of the Spirit of God. Jesus told His followers

they would face persecution because of Him. He said, "All men will hate you because of Me" **(Matt. 10:22)**. "If the head of the house has been called Beelzebub, how much more the members of His household" **(Matt. 10:25)**. "You will be handed over to be persecuted and put to death, and you will be hated by all nations because of Me. At that time many will turn away from the faith and will betray and hate each other, and many false prophets will appear and deceive many people" **(Matt. 24:9–12)**.

10. The seed that fell among thorns stands for those who hear, but as they go on their way they are choked by life's worries, riches, and pleasures, and they do not mature **(Luke 8:14)**.

11. The fourth kind of soil is the good soil—"The one who received the seed that fell on good soil is the man who hears the word and understands it. He produces a crop, yielding a hundred, sixty or thirty times what was sown" **(Matt. 13:23)**. Jesus calls those who hear and keep His Word blessed **(Luke 11:28)**. God's purpose for those who belong to Jesus is to live for Him **(2 Cor. 5:15)**.

12. God promises the following "fruit of faith": We will remain in God's love; we will obey His commands; our joy will be complete; we will be enabled to love one another as God in Christ has loved us.

## Other Parables of the King

Invite participants to read and reflect upon the meaning and content of the parables of Jesus included in this section. Ask participants to contribute their understanding of Jesus' words, "He who has ears, let him hear." Comment that Jesus' teaching requires faithful, believing recipients. Recipients of this type are persons in whom the Holy Spirit is working through the Word.

## A King without Honor

Read **Matt. 13:53–58** aloud to the group. The people in Jesus' hometown refused to believe in Him. "And He did not do many miracles there because of their lack of faith" **(v. 58)**.

# Applying the Message

Discuss this section as a large group.

1. Answers will vary. Possibilities include wealth, the cares and worries of the world around us, feelings of superior intellect, and self-sufficiency.

2. Accept participants' responses. God sows His seed in human hearts as His Word is preached, read, meditated upon, studied, sung, listened to, dramatized, and included in everyday conversations.

3. Samuel's response as he prepared to receive a message from God was, "Speak, for Your servant is listening" **(1 Samuel 3:10)**.

4. Accept participants' responses.

5–6. Invite participants to share their answers or insights and comments if they wish. God's power can enable us to overcome the weeds in our lives. We receive this power through the means of grace by the working of the Holy Spirit.

## Taking the Lesson Home

Urge interested participants to complete one or more of the suggested activities to reinforce and enrich the concepts taught in this lesson.

# Lesson 6

## Faith in the King (Matthew 14–18:14)

## Approaching This Study

Read aloud or invite a volunteer to read aloud the "Key verse" and the "Aim of this lesson."

## We Want to Believe

Read aloud and briefly discuss the opening story and accompanying information. Ask participants to share examples of childlike faith from their own experiences or about which they have heard.

## Working with the Text

### The Cost of Following the King

Begin by reading aloud Matthew's account of the death of John the Baptist. Mention that as the Holy Spirit enabled him, John courageously lived his faith, boldly speaking God's Law even though it cost him his life. Continue with the remaining portions of this section.

This lesson covers a large portion of Scripture. As suggested in previous lessons, you may wish to use various alternative methods so that you have time to address all the readings.

### The King Feeds 5,000 Hungry Subjects

Have a volunteer read **Matt. 14:13–21.** After the reading proceed with a discussion of the questions.

1. After Jesus heard about the death of John the Baptizer, He withdrew

by boat privately to a solitary place. But hearing of Jesus' departure, the crowds followed Him on foot.

2. As evening approached and it began to get late, the disciples approached Jesus and asked Him to send the crowds away, so they could go to the villages and buy themselves something to eat.

3. In response to Jesus' directive that the disciples feed the people, they listed their only resources as five loaves of bread and two fish. John's gospel identifies Andrew as the disciple who provided the information, adding that the loaves and fish belonged to a boy.

4. The people ate until they were satisfied. Twelve baskets of leftovers remained after the people were fed. The number of people who ate was about five thousand men, besides women and children.

## The King Walks on Water

Read or have one or more volunteers contribute to reading **Matt. 14:22–36** aloud. Read or paraphrase the introductory paragraph in the Study Guide to the group. Discuss the questions.

1. Alone and a considerable distance from the land, the disciples found themselves in a storm; their boat was buffeted by the waves because the wind was against it. The disciples remained in the storm until the fourth watch of the night (between 3 and 6 a.m.) when Jesus came to them walking on the water.

2. When the disciples saw Jesus walking on the lake, they were terrified. Thinking Jesus was a ghost, they cried out in fear.

3. Peter demonstrated his faith by asking Jesus if he, too, could walk on the water.

4. Peter began to sink when he saw the wind because He was afraid.

5. Jesus calmed the storm. John records that when Jesus got into the boat, the boat immediately reached the shore where they were heading. Some regard this as another miracle.

6. The disciples responded to the events they had witnessed by worshiping Jesus, saying, "Truly You are the Son of God."

## The King Teaches about Clean and Unclean

Read or invite one or two others to contribute to the reading of **Matt. 15:1–20** aloud. The Pharisees and teachers of the law trusted in the goodness they demonstrated by rigidly adhering to the tradition of the elders— a series of meticulous rules and regulations applied to everyday life. In focusing on these rules, they ignored the spirit of God's Law which is to love God and others wholeheartedly. Jesus plainly pointed out that outward obedience to rules is of no value when the person, working to elevate himself or herself through obedience, has an evil heart.

## The King of All People

Read or have a volunteer read aloud **Matt. 15:21–39**. Lead the group in a discussion of the questions that follow. Mention that the events recorded in these verses took place in the territory of Tyre and Sidon, north of Galilee, where many of the people knew of Jesus.

1. The woman wanted Jesus to heal her daughter who was suffering terribly from demon-possession.

2. She called Jesus *Lord* and the *Son of David* and asked Him to have mercy on her.

3. The woman responded to Jesus' testing by continuing to plead for His help.

4. The woman built on Jesus' comment, pointing out the privileged position in the household enjoyed by dogs who were pets. Her words evidence the depth of her faith in Jesus.

5. Jesus praised the woman's faith, adding that He had healed her daughter.

## The King is Challenged by His Critics

Continue with the reading and discussion of **Matt. 16:1–12**. Mention that Jesus' comment on the small amount of faith possessed by the disciples contrasts with His praise of the faith of the Canaanite woman.

## Who Is This King?

Read or involve one or more volunteers in the reading of **Matt. 16:13–28**. Continue with a discussion of the questions.

1. People thought Jesus was John the Baptizer (risen from the dead), Elijah, Jeremiah, or one of the prophets.

2. Peter identified Jesus as "the Christ, the Son of the living God."

3. Peter's confession means that, by faith, Jesus was recognized as the promised Son of God, the promised King of Israel, whose coming was foretold by Moses and the prophets.

4. The true church is built on Jesus Christ and on the teachings of the apostles and prophets.

5. Jesus specifically told His disciples that He must go to Jerusalem and suffer many things at the hands of the elders, chief priests, and teachers of the Law, and that He must be killed and on the third day be raised to life **(v. 21)**. Peter responded saying, "Never, Lord! This shall never happen to You!" **(v. 22)**. Jesus called Peter *Satan* because Peter's words echoed the desire of Satan, that Jesus would not fulfill the saving mission for which He was sent to earth. When Satan tempted Jesus with the promise to give Jesus all the kingdoms of the world, He was similarly trying to defer Jesus from His atoning suffering, death, and resurrection.

Conclude this section by reading or paraphasing the concluding paragraph in the Study Guide.

## The King Revealed

Read about and reflect upon the transfiguration of Christ **(Matt 17:1–13)**. Comment that in the transfiguration Jesus showed Himself to be the Promised One.

## The King's Power over Demons

Read **Matt. 17:14–21** aloud to the group. Continue with a discussion of the questions.

1. The man's son had seizures and was suffering greatly.

2. The disciples could not drive the demon out of the boy because of their lack of faith. Read the paragraph following this question to the group. Comment on the justifying and sanctifying power of God's gift of faith.

3. The mustard seed illustration includes the idea that God works great things through a person's faith. Faith grows and increases as the Holy Spirit works through God's Word.

## The King Teaches of His Kingdom

Read **Matt. 18:1–14** or involve volunteers in the reading of these verses to the group. Discuss the accompanying questions.

1. Those who are saved possess faith. Small children provide an excellent example of a powerless, sincere reliance upon others.

2. Those who are meek and poor in spirit trust in God for their sense of who they are, rather than in their own accomplishments or credentials.

3. Jesus told Nicodemus that he had to be born again **(John 3:3)**. Those who desire salvation must shed themselves of their perceived goodness and wisdom. Only in Christ can anyone find forgiveness, salvation, and goodness.

4. Jesus expressed concern that no one hamper or hinder the faith-life of those little ones who come to love and trust in Him.

5. God's people should support and encourage those who are weak in the faith, avoiding conduct that might lead them to doubt or question the working of God in the lives of those professing to be Christians.

6. *Eternal separation from God* means unending torment in hell.

7. Our salvation rests not in our own goodness but rather in the goodness Christ imparts to us by faith.

# Applying the Message

1. Encourage group responses, sharing one or two promises of God that are especially meaningful to you.

2. Again, encourage the group to open up by sharing your own doubts, how by God's help these struggles were overcome, and how God has enabled you to encourage others.

3. The Gentile woman did not give up but continued to ask God to grant her request even when He appeared not to be paying any attention to her.

4. Faith is the necessary element for all who enter into the kingdom of God. God promises that whoever believes in Jesus will not perish but will have eternal life.

5. As you accept the responses of the group, point out that we can prepare ourselves by having ready a short, concise, and personal statement of what we believe about Jesus Christ.

6. Only Jesus saves. God's Word clearly identifies Jesus as the only means to salvation **(Acts 4:12).**

## Taking the Lesson Home

Urge interested participants to complete one or more of the suggested activities to reinforce and enrich the concepts taught in this lesson.

# Lesson 7

## Forgive as the King Forgives
## (Matthew 18:15–19:15)

## Approaching This Study

Read aloud or invite a volunteer to read aloud the "Key verses" and the "Aim of this lesson."

## We Need to Forgive

Read aloud and briefly discuss the opening story and accompanying information. Ask, **Why is it so difficult to forgive one another?**

## Working with the Text

Work through this portion of the lesson in small groups, or consider each section as a whole group.

### Greatest in the Kingdom

Read or invite a volunteer to read **Matt. 18:15–20** aloud to the group.

Then continue with a discussion of the questions included in this section.

1. Jesus said, "If your brother sins against you, go and show him his fault, just between the two of you. If he listens to you, you have won your brother over" **(Matt. 15:16).** Underscore that in this context the term *brother* refers to fellow believers.

2. The motive of the confrontation should be to love our fellow believers because of our love for God **(1 John 4:19–21)** and to restore the erring brother **(Gal. 6:1).**

3. Taking along one or two other people will help to keep communication going as the problem is discussed. Rarely is a problem all one-sided. An impartial observer can "keep both parties honest" with each other as they talk out their hurts and their differences.

4. If the erring person still refuses to listen, the third step is to tell the matter to the church. If the person refuses to listen to the church, such a person is to be treated as an unbeliever.

5. Jesus promises to bless with His presence even the assembly of two or three gathered together in His name. To gather together in Jesus' name means to enjoy the fellowship of other believers.

6. Christ gives the church the authority to forgive or to withhold forgiveness in His name.

7. Faith opens the door to the kingdom of heaven. Sin and unbelief close the door to the kingdom of heaven.

## The King Teaches More about Forgiveness

Read the introductory paragraph in this section to the group. Then continue by reading or asking one or two others to participate in reading **Matt. 18:21–35.** Proceed with the questions.

1. The forgiveness the people of God offer to others should not be limited to any specific number of times, just as God continues to forgive us day after day.

2. His debt was due and he was unable to pay. Since he was unable to pay his debt, the king had the right to confiscate the debtor's property and to sell the debtor and his family into slavery. Hence, the debtor was entirely at the mercy of the king.

3. This same servant threw the person owing him a relatively small debt into prison. This action showed the heart of the forgiven man to be unappreciative and evil.

4. The king took back his forgiveness and turned the debtor over to the jailers to be tortured until he could pay back all he owed.

5. Jesus said, "This is how My heavenly Father will treat each of you unless you forgive your brother from your heart" **(Matt. 18:35).**

6. The debt each of us owe our heavenly Father is the debt we have accumulated because of our sinfulness. Because of our natural sinfulness, none of us can ever merit or earn God's forgiveness. Because Jesus, the Lamb of God, has taken away the sin of the world (**John 1:29**), God the Father shows His mercy to us, blotting out our transgressions and remembering our sins no more (**Is. 43:25**). Just as Jesus healed and forgave the sins of the man sick with palsy (**Matt. 9:2**), He has made us alive in Him (**Col. 2:13**), making it possible for us to rejoice in the reconciliation with God, eternal life, and salvation that are ours in Him (**Rom. 5:11**).

God the Father expects us to forgive others as we have been forgiven (**Matt. 6:12; Col. 3:13; Eph 4:32**), demonstrating mercy just as we have received mercy at the hand of God (**Luke 6:36**).

7. Withholding mercy and forgiveness shows a lack of faith in God and ingratitude toward Him.

## The King Teaches about Relationships

Read or invite one or more participants to read **Matt. 19:1–15.** Read or paraphrase for the group the information in the paragraph preceding item one. Continue with a discussion of the questions in this section.

1. Jesus directs the Pharisees to find the answer to their question in the Word of God.

2. Jesus describes marriage saying, "So they are no longer two, but one. Therefore what God has joined together, let man not separate" (**v. 6**).

3. Jesus says that divorce was permitted, not because it was part of God's plan, but because of the sinful hardening of the human heart. The marriage bond is broken when marital unfaithfulness has occurred. Read the comments in the lesson about the disciples' response to Jesus' teaching.

4. God would have those who love and trust in Him submit to one another out of reverence for Christ. Wives are to submit to their husbands, and husbands are to love their wives as their own bodies, giving themselves for their wives just as Christ loved and gave Himself for the church.

5. The forgiveness that we have in Christ is the basis for the unconditional love, continual forgiveness, and mutual submission God would have married persons demonstrate toward one another.

6. Jesus says that the kingdom of heaven belongs to those who are like children. Childlike qualities include the ability to trust and the ability to admit helplessness. As the Holy Spirit gives us the gift of faith, He enables us to seek and receive the forgiveness God offers freely in Christ Jesus, our Lord.

## Applying the Message

1–5. Invite participants to comment on one or more of these questions after they have worked through them individually. Affirm the motivation and power God provides through the means of grace. Point out that truly receiving and giving forgiveness happens only by the grace of God through the working of the Holy Spirit.

## Taking the Lesson Home

Urge interested participants to complete one or both of the suggested activities to reinforce and enrich the concepts taught in this lesson.

# Lesson 8

## Serve the King (Matthew 19:16–23:39)

## Approaching This Study

Read aloud or invite a volunteer to read aloud the "Key verses" and the "Aim of this lesson."

## We Want to Be Great

Read aloud and briefly discuss the opening story. Stress how Jesus became the servant of all through His life, death, and resurrection on our behalf. Ask participants to give examples of persons whose lives of service to God and others evidence the love of Jesus at work within them.

## Working with the Text

Approach the large portion of Scripture, choosing from among the options previously suggested.

### The King Talks about Earning Eternal Life

Read or ask a volunteer to read **Matt. 19:16–30.** Discuss the questions referring to this portion of the text.

1. Answers may vary somewhat. Jesus referred the rich man to the Fifth Commandment (Do not murder), the Sixth Commandment (Do not commit adultery), the Seventh Commandment (Do not steal), the Eighth Commandment (Do not give false testimony), and the Fourth Commandment (Honor your father and mother). Jesus added, "Love your neighbor as

yourself," which serves either as a summary of the second table of the Law or as a reference to the Ninth and Tenth Commandments.

2. Jesus said, "If you love Me, you will obey what I command" **(John 14:15).**

3. It appears he had endeavored to lead a decent, upright life.

4. Jesus described the first and greatest Commandment, "Love the Lord your God with all your heart and with all your soul and with all your mind" **(Matt. 22:37).** God had not become the center and focus of his life and actions.

5. Wealth and possessions received a higher priority in this man's life than God and the things of God.

6. "People who want to get rich fall into temptation and a trap and into many foolish and harmful desires that plunge men into ruin and destruction. For the love of money is a root of all kinds of evil. Some people, eager for money, have wandered from the faith and pierced themselves with many griefs" (**1 Tim. 6:9–10**).

7. Jesus promised great rewards to those who in faith give Him the highest place in their lives, concluding with the promise that many who are first will be last and many who are last will be first. God's value system differs from that of the world. Only faith in Christ merits a place in glory.

## The King Tells a Parable

Continue with a reading and a discussion of **Matt. 20:1–16.** Here our Lord offers a parable in response to Peter's question, "What then will there be for us?"

1. The landowner is God, and the hired men are those who, by faith, enter the kingdom of God.

2. God rewards according to His goodness and worthiness, not according to our own, giving eternal life to all who believe in His Son as their Savior.

3. Work in the kingdom of God is the privilege He provides to all to whom He has given the gift of faith.

## The King Speaks of Greatness

Proceed as previously, reading and discussing **Matt. 20:17–28.**

1. The mother of James and John asked Jesus if one her sons might sit at His right hand and the other at His left. Perhaps she expected Jesus to establish an earthly kingdom in which He would free Israel of their foreign oppressors.

2. Most likely they saw this as an attempt on the part of the mother of James and John to move them into a privileged position over the rest of the Twelve.

3. The term *cup* is sometimes used in Scripture to refer to sorrow and suffering.

4. The Gentiles saw greatness in terms of the positions of authority that the rulers held over people. In contrast to this natural human understanding of greatness, Jesus put forth the following: "Instead, whoever wants to become great among you must be your servant, and whoever wants to be first must be your slave—just as the Son of Man did not come to be served, but to serve, and to give His life as a ransom for many" **(Matt. 20:26–28).**

5. Jesus comforted the grieving **(John 11:17–27)**, He washed His disciples' feet **(John 13:1–17)**, He saw to the care of His mother **(John 19:25–27)**, and He healed those who were sick.

6. Jesus suffered and died, giving His life in payment for the sins of the world.

## The King, Son of David

Read and discuss **Matt. 20:29–34** and the questions that follow.

1. Jesus was the descendant of King David, the Promised Messiah whose almighty power would defeat even death.

2. Possible answers include helping, caring for, and meeting the expressed needs of others. As Jesus cares for others, we, His followers, demonstrate His love and concern for those in need by giving of ourselves and of our possessions.

## The King Enters

Continue with the reading and discussing of **Matt. 21:1–11.**

1. The disciples followed Jesus' instructions and brought a donkey and a colt for Him to ride upon. They placed their cloaks on the back of these animals as a make-shift saddle for Jesus. Some people in the crowd spread their cloaks on the road before Jesus while others cut branches from the trees and spread them on the road. The crowds shouted, "Hosanna to the Son of David! Blessed is He who comes in the name of the Lord! Hosanna in the highest!"

2. Old Testament prophets foretold that the inhabitants of Jerusalem would welcome in praise the Savior who would enter riding a donkey and her colt.

3. The crowds proclaimed Jesus as the Son of David, the promised Messiah. Comment that the honor that came to Jesus on Palm Sunday was humbly bestowed **(Zech. 9:9)** as befitting the Servant King.

## The King's Temple

Read and discuss **Matt. 21:12–22** using the questions provided in the Study Guide.

1. People were buying and selling in the outer court of the temple. Quoting **Jer. 7:11,** Jesus told the people they had dishonored God's house, regarding it as a den of robbers.

2. The children in the temple shouted, "Hosanna to the Son of David."

3. God's Word talks about the lips of children and infants praising God **(Psalm 8:2).** Surely God is pleased when believers of all ages honor Him with their worship and praise.

4. Martha tended to Jesus' physical needs and comforts while Mary served God by hearing His Word.

## Questioning the King's Authority

Read **Matt. 21:23–27** aloud to the group. Lead them in a discussion of the questions provided for this section in the Study Guide.

1. The chief priests and the elders of the people asked Jesus by what authority He performed His ministry.

2. Jesus' counterquestion concerned the ministry of John the Baptizer. He asked whether John's authority came from heaven or from men. "They discussed it among themselves and said, 'If we say, from heaven, He will ask, then why didn't you believe in him? But if we say, from men—we are afraid of the people, for they all hold that John was a prophet'" **(vv. 25b–26).**

3. If they had believed that John had been sent to them by God, they would have repented.

## More Parables from the King

Choose three volunteers. Ask each to read one of the three parables in this section—the Parable of the Two Sons **(Matt. 21:28–32),** the Parable of the Tenants **(Matt. 21:33–46),** and the Parable of the Wedding Banquet **(Matt. 22:1–14).**

1. These parables were initially addressed to the chief priests and the Pharisees.

2. The son who agreed to go to work in the vineyard represents the self-righteous who, though appearing to be the people of God, refuse His calling. The son who at first refused to work in the vineyard, but later changed his mind and went, represents sinners who repent.

3. He calls those who hear Him to repentance and faith.

4. The landowner is God. The tenants are the Jews or their leaders. The son is Christ.

5. Jesus is the stone rejected by the builders which has become the capstone. Rejected by the recognized leaders of the church of His day, Jesus became the capstone—the foundation—of the only true and saving faith.

6. Jesus said the kingdom will be taken away from them and given to

those who would receive it.

7. "They looked for a way to arrest Him, but they were afraid of the crowd because the people held that He was a prophet" **(Matt. 21:46).**

8. All who possess the "wedding clothes" of faith in Jesus will be saved.

## Enemies Attempt to Trap the King

Mention to the group that this section includes three attempts to trap Jesus in His own words. Again, choose three volunteers. Ask one volunteer to read each of the following portions of this section from God's Word: **Matt. 22:15–22, 23–33, 34–45.** Continue with a discussion of the questions.

1. When asked whether or not it was right to pay taxes to Caesar, Jesus identified the goal of the Pharisees to trap Jesus. He distinguished between Caesar and God. Christians serve the government by submitting in willing obedience to the laws of the land while adhering to the higher authority of God.

2. The Sadducees denied the resurrection. Comment that the Sadducees attempted to succeed where the Pharisees failed—in attempting to make Jesus appear to be a fool.

3. When God called Himself the God of Abraham, the God of Isaac, and the God of Jacob, He was referring to these men as believers who, though long dead, were alive in glory. Jesus used the very sacred writing adhered to by the Sadducees to prove the resurrection.

4. The motivation to serve God and man originates in wholehearted devotion, which is the gift of the Holy Spirit.

5. All Commandments are kept in showing love for God and love for others.

6. Jesus Christ is both true man (David's Son) and true God (David's Lord).

7. David, like the other authors of portions of the Bible, spoke by inspiration of the Holy Spirit.

## The King Proclaims Seven Woes

Arrange for **Matt. 23:1–39** to be read aloud. Then continue with a discussion of the questions.

1. Jesus said of the Pharisees, "Everything they do is done for men to see" **(Matt. 23:5).**

2. Examples cited by Jesus include the following: they make their phylacteries wide and the tassels on their garments long; they love the place of honor at banquets and the most important seats in the synagogues; they love to be greeted in the marketplaces and to have men call them "Rabbi" **(vv. 5–7).**

3. Jesus said, "The greatest among you will be your servant. For whoever exalts himslef will be humbled, and whoever humbles himself will be exalted" (vv. 11–12).

4. Jesus condemns the religious leaders for their hypocrisy.

5. Specific acts of disservice to the kingdom of God include the following: shutting the kingdom of heaven in men's faces; traveling over land and sea to win a single convert, and when he becomes one, making him twice as self-righteous and wrongly self-secure as they are; saying that if anyone swears by the temple, it means nothing, but if anyone swears by the gold of the temple, he is bound by his oath; giving a tenth of their spices but neglecting the more important matters of the law—justice, mercy, and faithfulness; being full of greed and self-indulgence; appearing righteous while full of hypocrisy and wickedness; saying they would not have taken part in the shedding of the prophets' blood if they had been alive in the days of their forefathers when they, too, are murderers of those sent from God.

6. Jesus refers to a hen gathering her chicks under her wings as a picture of the salvation with which He desires to bless all people. The emotion Jesus demonstrates here is one of grief over those who reject Him.

## Applying the Message

This portion of the lesson is provided for the participants' personal reflection. Invite participants to share with the group any comments or insights they may have.

## Taking the Lesson Home

Urge interested participants to complete one or more of the suggested activities to reinforce and enrich the concepts taught in this lesson.

# Lesson 9

## Inheriting the Kingdom (Matthew 24–25)

## Approaching This Study

Read aloud or invite a volunteer to read aloud the "Key verses" and the "Aim of this lesson."

# We Need to Look Forward

Read aloud and briefly discuss the opening story. Ask, **From what you know or have heard about life in the latter days, what evidence can you cite indicating that Jesus is coming soon?** After a few moments of discussion, read aloud the final paragraphs of this section.

# Working with the Text

This section of each lesson covers a large portion of Scripture. You may wish to use one of the previously suggested methods to cover the Scripture readings.

### The King Tells about His Return

Read or involve one or more volunteers in reading **Matt. 24:1–51** aloud to the group. Then discuss the questions that follow.

1. Jesus and His disciples were discussing the coming destruction of Jerusalem.

2. Jesus predicted that not one stone of the temple would be left on another; every one of them would be thrown down. The disciples privately questioned Jesus about two topics—the destruction of Jerusalem and the coming of the end of the age. Famines and earthquakes are signs of the coming of the end of all things. Signs among believers include the following: many will come, claiming to be the Christ; there will be wars and rumors of wars, persecution and hatred of Christians, widespread falling away, false prophets, an increase of wickedness; the Gospel will be preached to the whole world; the abomination that causes desolation will stand in the holy place; for the sake of the elect the days of distress and wickedness will be cut short. Jesus warns against being deceived by false prophets and by those claiming to be the Christ.

3. Jesus promises His followers that those who stand firm to the end will be saved and that the Gospel will be preached in the whole world as a testimony to all nations. Then the end will come **(vv. 13–14)**.

4. The destruction to occur will be complete and total and it will happen suddenly.

5. **Is. 13:10** tells of a darkening of the stars, the sun, and the moon associated with the coming of the day of the Lord. They who have refused to believe in Jesus as the Son of God and Savior of the world will mourn.

6. On the Last Day Jesus will send His angels with a loud trumpet call, and they will gather His elect from the four winds, from one end of the heavens to the other **(Matt. 24:31)**.

7. Jesus describes the lesson of the fig tree as follows: "As soon as its twigs get tender and its leaves come out, you know that summer is near"

(**v. 32**). As we witness the predicted signs in the world around us, we know that the end of all things is ever nearer.

8. Jesus said, "Heaven and earth will pass away, but My words will never pass away" (**v. 35**).

9. **Verse 36** indicates that no one except for God the Father knows the exact day and hour on which Jesus will come again. According to His human nature, Jesus does not know when the end of all things will occur.

10. The people of Noah's day went on with their lives as though nothing would ever happen to change the regular course of events, but one day the flood came and they were destroyed.

11. If a homeowner were to find out exactly when a thief would come, he or she could be ready for the thief.

12. Jesus instructs His followers to be ready at all times for His coming.

13. The wise and faithful servant has been put in charge of the other servants with the instructions to give them their food at the proper times. When the master returns, he will find the faithful servant busy following his directives. The wicked servant begins to beat his follow servants and to eat and drink with drunkards, unconcerned and unprepared for his master's return.

## More Parables from the King

Read or involve volunteers in the reading of the Parable of the Ten Virgins (**Matthew 25:1–13**) and the Parable of the Talents (**Matthew 25:14–30**) to the group. Discuss the questions that follow each.

1. Jesus' coming is represented in this parable by a bridegroom whose arrival is awaited by ten young women. Five of them have brought along an adequate supply of oil. Five of them did not bring along enough oil and, as a consequence, could not take part in the wedding banquet.

2. The words of the bridegroom to the young women without oil ("I don't know you") are an echo of **Matt. 7:23.** On the Last Day, Jesus will recognize only those with faith in Him as qualifying for eternal life.

3. Single words to describe the main lesson of this parable may vary. Possibilities include *watch*, *prepare*, and *anticipate*.

4. The master is God, and the servants are those professing to believe in Him. The master expects those who belong to Him to work for the advancement of His interests. The first two servants are commended for the fruit of their efforts and are given increased responsibilities. The man who did nothing with what was given to him is called wicked and lazy and is thrown out into the darkness where there will be weeping and gnashing of teeth.

5. God expects those of us who belong to Him to evidence His presence

in our lives by doing His work while we await His coming to take us to live with Him in glory.

## When the King Comes Again

Read or ask a volunteer to read **Matt. 25:31–46** aloud to the group. Discuss the questions that follow.

1. In His First Coming Jesus arrived in humility; when He arrives the second time He will sit on His throne in heavenly glory. When He was born at Bethlehem, His coming was not at first widely heralded; when Jesus comes to judge the world, all nations will be gathered before Him.

2. All people will be present on the Last Day.

3. John records Jesus' description of His sheep: "My sheep listen to My voice; I know them, and they follow Me. I give them eternal life, and they shall never perish; no one can snatch them out of My hand" **(John 10:27–28)**.

4. Whoever believes in the Son has eternal life, but whoever rejects the Son will not see life, for God's wrath remains on him **(John 3:36)**.

5. Jesus will judge the world on the Last Day.

6. To believers Jesus will say, "Come, you who are blessed by my Father; take your inheritance, the kingdom prepared for you since the creation of the world. For I was hungry and you gave Me something to eat, I was thirsty and you gave Me something to drink, I was a stranger and you invited Me in, I needed clothes and you clothed Me, I was sick and you looked after Me, I was in prison and you came to visit Me" **(Matt. 25:34–36)**.

7. Jesus refers to the kingdom of heaven as an inheritance. Inheritances are not earned; rather they are bestowed on persons by virtue of a preestablished relationship. In this case, we inherit eternal life because we are the children of God through faith in Christ Jesus.

8. God the Father has been preparing our inheritance for us since the creation of the world **(v. 34)**.

9. Works evidence that a saving faith in Jesus is alive in the person doing them.

10. Through the working of the Holy Spirit, faith is demonstrated in the lives of believers in their words, attitudes, and actions. Jesus said, "Then the righteous will answer Him, 'Lord, when did we see You hungry and feed You, or thirsty and give You something to drink? When did we see You a stranger and invite You in, or needing clothes and clothe You? When did we see You sick or in prison and go to visit You?' The King will reply, 'I tell you the truth, whatever you did for one of the least of these brothers of Mine, you did for Me'" **(Matt. 25:37–40)**.

11. The most terrible words a person can ever hear are these: "Depart from Me, you who are cursed, into the eternal fire prepared for the devil and his angels. For I was hungry and you gave Me nothing to eat, I was thirsty and you gave Me nothing to drink, I was a stranger and you did not invite Me in, I needed clothes and you did not clothe Me, I was sick and in prison and you did not look after Me" **(Matt. 25:41b–43)**.

12. Without faith it is impossible to please God **(Heb. 11:6)**.

13. The separation from God and torment in hell will endure forever. Hell was the place to which the evil angels were sent after they fell into sin. We know God does not want people to be eternally lost because He specifically says so in His Word **(Ez. 33:11; 2 Peter 3:9)**.

14. Heaven is a place where God will fill us with joy in His presence and with eternal pleasures at His right hand **(Ps. 16:11)**, where we will live in the presence of Christ **(John 14:1–3)**, where a great multitude from every nation, tribe, and people will assemble before the throne of the Lamb to serve God day and night in perfect comfort and happiness **(Rev. 7:9–17; 21:1–4)**.

## Applying the Message

1. Affirm responses that demonstrate a confidence in our salvation by grace through faith in Christ Jesus, our Lord.

2. Welcome participants' responses. Share examples of your own to encourage sharing.

3. Invite someone to read **2 Peter 3:3–13** aloud to the group. Encourage comments. Stress that although many years have passed since the end of the world was foretold, it will come. God promises to equip and fortify those who belong to Him so that we may meet Him when He comes, confident in His love and anticipating the reward that awaits us through the merits of Christ.

4. Invite anyone who wishes to comment to do so. Underscore the working of the Holy Spirit through God's Word and the sacraments to bring people to, and preserve them in, the saving faith.

## Taking the Lesson Home

Urge interested participants to complete one or more of the suggested activities to reinforce and enrich the concepts taught in this lesson.

# Lesson 10

## The King Commands Us to Share the Kingdom
## (Matthew 26–28)

### Approaching This Study

Read aloud or invite a volunteer to read aloud the "Key verses" and the "Aim of this lesson."

### We Need to Tell

Read aloud and invite participants to comment on this introductory section.

### Working with the Text

This section covers the last three chapters of **Matthew.** Consider varying your approach using one of the suggestions provided in previous sessions.

#### The Plot Against the King

Read aloud **Matt. 26:1–13** and the introductory material in the Study Guide. Then discuss the questions that follow.

1. She came to Jesus with a jar of very expensive perfume which she poured on His head as He was reclining at the table. John's gospel records that she poured the perfume on Jesus' feet and wiped His feet with her hair and that the house was filled with the fragrance of the perfume. Mary is also remembered for sitting at Jesus' feet and listening to Him. **(Luke 10:39).**

2. Jesus said, "When she poured this perfume on My body, she did it to prepare Me for burial" **(v. 12).** Mary's act of worship demonstrated her love, faith, and gratitude to God for the free gift of salvation He was about to earn at a very high price.

#### The King Is Betrayed

Read or invite a participant to read **Matt. 26:14–25** aloud to the class. Continue with a review of the discussion questions.

1. **John 12:5** identifies Judas Iscariot as being critical of the use of the expensive perfume to anoint Jesus. Judas asked, "Why wasn't this perfume sold and the money given to the poor? It was worth a year's wages." John adds that Judas said this, not because he cared about the poor, but because he was a thief. About Jesus' betrayal, Scriptures prophesied the following:

"Even My close friend, whom I trusted, he who shared My bread, has lifted up his heel against Me" **(Ps. 41:9).**

"I told them, 'If you think it best, give me my pay; but if not, keep it.' So they paid me thirty pieces of silver. And the Lord said to me, 'Throw it to the potter'—the handsome price at which they priced me! So I took the thirty pieces of silver and threw them into the house of the Lord to the potter" **(Zech. 11:12–13).**

2. Jesus spoke about the upcoming betrayal, warning Judas as if urging him to repentance.

## The King Shares a Meal with His Subjects

Read **Matt. 26:26–30** and the first paragraph in this section to the group. As you consider the question at the end of the paragraph, have a volunteer read **Heb. 9:11–14** aloud. Jesus' words of institution at the taking of the cup were, "This is the blood of the covenant, which is poured out for many for the forgiveness of sins" **(v. 28). Heb. 9:11–14** refers to Jesus' sacrifice as the once and for all payment for the sins of the world. Continue reading the last paragraph in this section.

## The King Grieves

Continue with **Matt. 26:31–46,** using the same approach as in the previous section.

1. Jesus foretold both the disciples' desertion of Him and Peter's denial.

2. Jesus promised that after His resurrection, He would go ahead of the disciples into Galilee.

3. Jesus needed the strength that only His heavenly Father could provide. He was sorrowful and troubled. He said, "My soul is overwhelmed with sorrow to the point of death" **(v. 38).**

4. Sorrow and trouble are part of the human experience. Yet Jesus did not give in to temptation. Instead, He brought His grief and burdens to His loving, heavenly Father in prayer.

5. Jesus' concern for Peter focused not on the physical strength Peter would derive from resting, but rather on the spiritual strength Peter would need very shortly.

## The King Is Arrested

Continue with the reading and discussing of **Matt. 26:47–56.**

1. Jesus called Judas, "Friend."

2. **Verses 50–56** indicate that Jesus willingly went along with those who arrested Him. John adds that Jesus identified Himself as the one they wanted.

## The King Is Tried and Disowned

Continue with the reading and discussing of **Matt. 26:57–75.** Mention that this section covers the night trial of Jesus and Peter's denial.

1. **Verse 59** records that the leaders of the people had predetermined to find Jesus guilty of something so that they might put Him to death.

2. **Is. 53:7** describes the behavior of Jesus at the trial as follows: "He was oppressed and afflicted, yet He did not open His mouth; He was led like a lamb to the slaughter, and as a sheep before her shearers is silent, so he did not open His mouth."

3. Jesus' description of Himself seated at the right hand of the Mighty One coming on the clouds of heaven is reminiscent of **Ps. 110:1,** "The Lord says to my Lord: 'Sit at My right hand until I make Your enemies a footstool for Your feet'" and of **Daniel 7:13,** which says, "In my vision at night I looked, and there before me was One like a Son of Man, coming with the clouds of heaven. He approached the Ancient of Days and was led into His presence."

4. That Jesus would be mocked, spit upon, and struck are all foretold in **Isaiah.**

5. Jesus told Peter He had prayed for him. Later, after Peter's denial, Jesus glanced at Peter, and Peter realized what he had done.

## The King's Betrayer Commits Suicide and the King Is Tried

Continue as previously with the next section, **Matt. 27:1–26.** Mention that Jesus was brought to Pilate, the Roman governor, for trial because the Jewish court was not allowed to carry out the death penalty.

1. The difference between Peter's sorrow over sin and that of Judas is illustrated by **2 Cor. 7:10,** "Godly sorrow brings repentance that leads to salvation and leaves no regret, but worldly sorrow brings death." Both Peter and Judas realized they had sinned. Peter turned to Jesus and the forgiveness He freely offers; Judas turned to despair and hanged himself.

2. Before Pilate, the elders of the people accused Jesus, saying, "We have found this man subverting our nation. He opposes payment of taxes to Caesar and claims to be Christ, a king" **(Luke 23:1–2).**

3. While Jesus answered yes to Pilate's question about whether He was the king of the Jews, He gave no reply to the false accusations of the chief priests and elders.

4. Pilate sought to free Jesus by asking the people to choose between Jesus and Barabbas, by sending Jesus to Herod, by seeking to appease the people's hatred of Jesus through punishing Him, and by dramatically washing his hands in front of Jesus' accusers.

## The King Is Killed

Continue as previously to cover **Matt. 27:27–54.**

1. Referring to His death on the cross, Jesus said, "Just as Moses lifted up the snake in the desert, so the Son of Man must be lifted up, that everyone who believes in Him may have eternal life" **(John 3:14–15).**

2. Other verses from the Old Testament foreshadowing the crucifixion include the following:

"...A band of evil men has encircled Me, they have pierced My hands and My feet" **(Ps. 22:16).**

"They divide My garments among them and cast lots for My clothing" **(Ps. 22:18).**

"They put gall in My food and gave Me vinegar for My thirst" **(Ps. 69:21).**

"...He poured out His life unto death, and was numbered with the transgressors. For He bore the sin of many, and made intercession for the transgressors" **(Is. 53:12).**

3. The following mark the uniqueness of Jesus' crucifixion: darkness came over the whole land during the last three hours before Jesus' death; at the death of Jesus the curtain of the temple was torn in two from top to bottom; the earth shook and the rocks split when Jesus died; the tombs broke open and the bodies of many holy people who had died were raised to life; the terrified centurion exclaimed, "Surely He was the Son of God!" Answers may vary somewhat.

4. See item three.

## The King is Buried

Read and discuss **Matt. 27:55–66.** About Jesus' burial, Isaiah prophesied, "He was assigned a grave with the wicked, and with the rich in His death, though He had done no violence, nor was any deceit in His mouth" **(Is. 53:9).**

## The King Rises from the Dead

Proceed as previously with the next portion of the text, **Matt. 28:1–15.** Read the introductory paragraph aloud to the group.

1. The words of the angel to the women indicate that the women must have been frightened **(v. 5).**

2. Luke records that the disciples "did not believe the women, because their words seemed to them like nonsense" **(Luke 24:11).**

3. "...some of the guards went into the city and reported to the chief priests everything that had happened **(28:11).**

4. After His resurrection, Jesus appeared to the women **(28:9),** to the Emmaus disciples, Simon Peter, and the Eleven **(Luke 24:10, 13–15, 34,**

**36)**, to the disciples still another time in Jerusalem **(John 20:26)**, to more than 500 believers, to James, to all the apostles, and last of all, to Paul **(1 Corinthians 15:6–8)**.

## The King's Commission

Read to the group **Matt. 28:16–20** and the introductory paragraph in this section. Continue with the discussion questions.

1. "Then Jesus came to them and said, 'All authority in heaven and on earth has been given to Me. Therefore go and make disciples of all nations, baptizing them in the name of the Father and of the Son and of the Holy Spirit, and teaching them to obey everything I have commanded you. And surely I am with you always, to the very end of the age' " **(vv. 18–20)**.

2. Jesus commissioned His followers with His power and authority. Jesus said, "All authority in heaven and on earth has been given to Me" **(v. 18)**.

3. The task of discipling involves using the means of grace to bring people to, and sustain them in, the saving faith in Jesus. Discipling occurs through baptizing and teaching.

4. We are claimed in Baptism by our heavenly Father who in His love created and sustains us, by the Son who gave His life in our place, and by the Holy Spirit who keeps us in the faith. The name of God into which we are baptized identifies the triune nature of God.

5. Jesus promises to always remain with us **(Matt. 28:20)**.

## Applying the Message

Invite participants to reflect privately on the items in this section. Welcome insights or comments from the group.

## Taking the Lesson Home

Urge interested participants to complete one or both of the suggested activities to reinforce and enrich the concepts taught in this lesson.

Find Healing in . . .

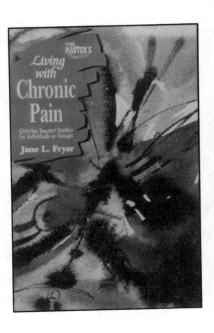

J esus' healing touch of love, hope
and forgiveness will help you find
positive solutions to the concerns
weighing on your heart. As you study
and share His Word, the Holy Spirit
will lead you to grow in spiritual
maturity and deeper faith experiences, and even reach out to those
who face similar needs and concerns.

*Four to five sessions each*

Living with **Chronic Pain**
Suffering from **Guilt**
Living with **Change**
Coping with **Compassion Fatigue**

Living with **Compulsive Behaviors**
Discovering **Life after Divorce**
Living with **Infertility**
Surviving **Sexual Abuse**

3558 SOUTH JEFFERSON AVENUE
SAINT LOUIS, MISSOURI 63118-3968

© CPH 1994   H54920/2